Classical Masterpieces

I CAN PLAY THAT!

Published by
Wise Publications
part of The Music Sales Group
14-15 Berners Street, London W1D 3JB, UK.

Exclusive Distributors:
Music Sales Limited
Distribution Centre, Newmarket Road,
Bury St Edmunds, Suffolk IP33 3YB, UK.
Music Sales Corporation
257 Park Avenue South, New York,
NY 10010, USA.
Music Sales Pty Limited
20 Resolution Drive, Caringbah, NSW 2229, Australia.

Order No. AM92106
ISBN 0-7119-4232-3
This book © Copyright 2005 Wise Publications,
a division of Music Sales Limited.

www.musicsales.com

Your Guarantee of Quality
As publishers, we strive to produce every book to the highest
commercial standards. This book has been carefully designed to
minimise awkward page turns and to make playing from it a real
pleasure. Particular care has been given to specifying acid-free,
neutral-sized paper made from pulps which have not been elemental
chlorine bleached. This pulp is from farmed sustainable forests and
was produced with special regard for the environment. Throughout, the
printing and binding have been planned to ensure a sturdy, attractive
publication which should give years of enjoyment. If your copy fails to
meet our high standards, please inform us and we will gladly replace it.

Air On A G String

Music by Johann Sebastian Bach

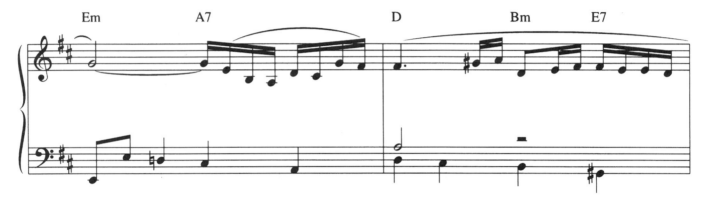

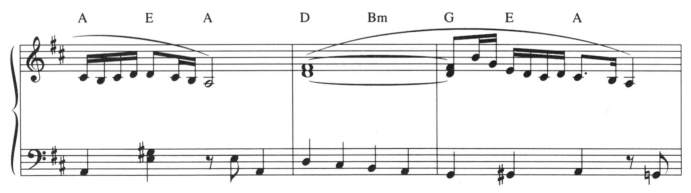

Bourrée

Music by Johann Sebastian Bach

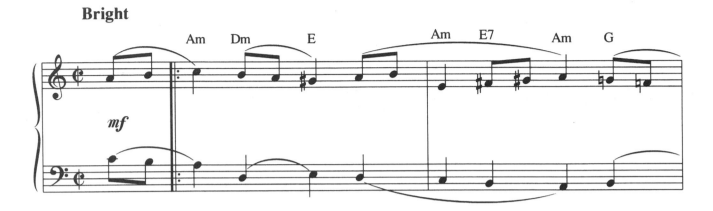

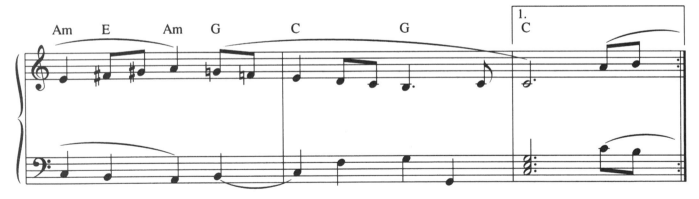

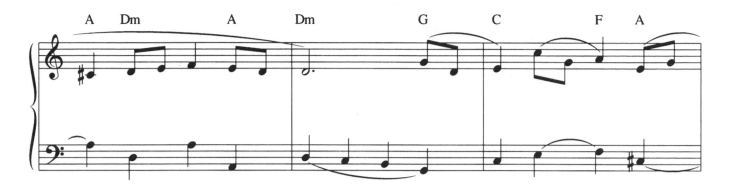

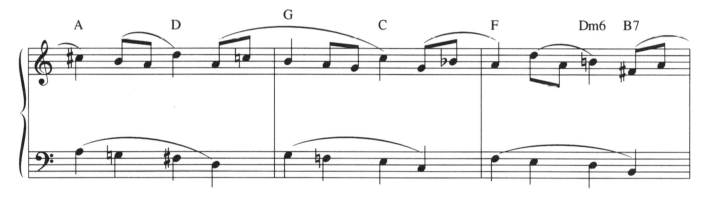

In Tears Of Grief
(from *St Matthew Passion*)

Music by Johann Sebastian Bach

Moderately

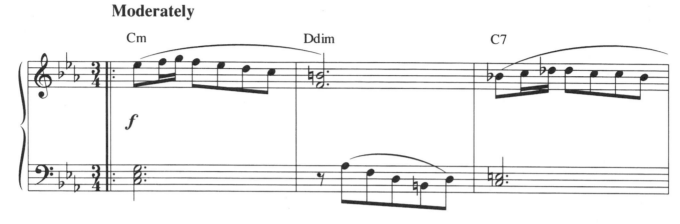

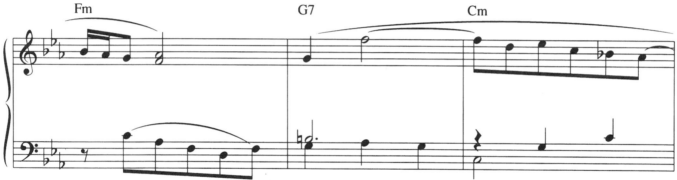

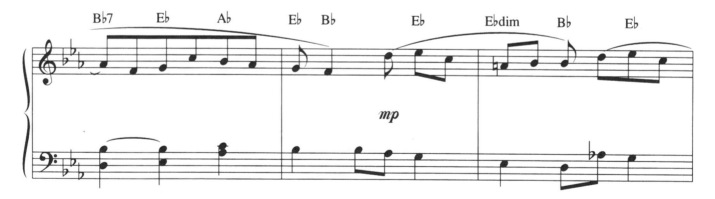

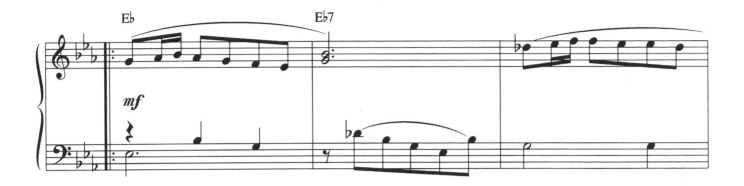

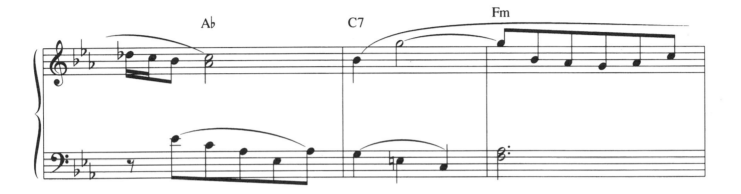

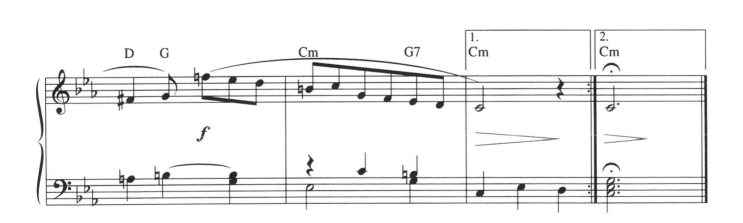

Minuet In B Minor
(from *Orchestral Suite No.2*)

Music by Johann Sebastian Bach

Moderately

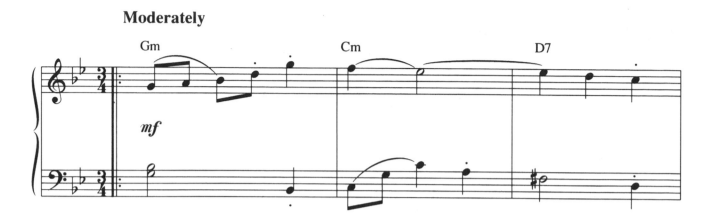

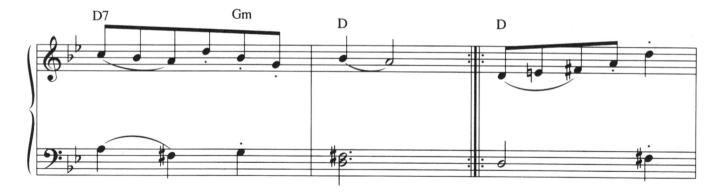

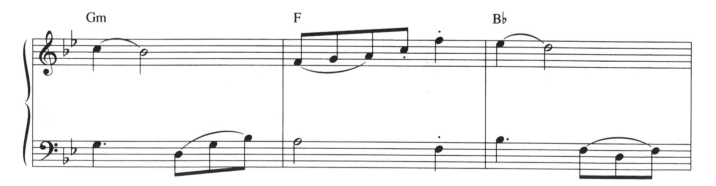

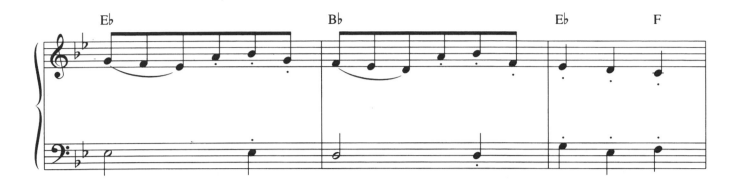

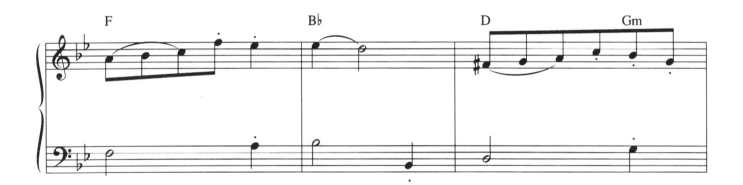

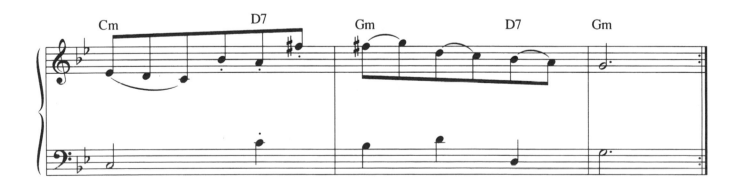

Minuet In D Minor

Music by Johann Sebastian Bach

Moderately

Minuet In G

Music by Johann Sebastian Bach

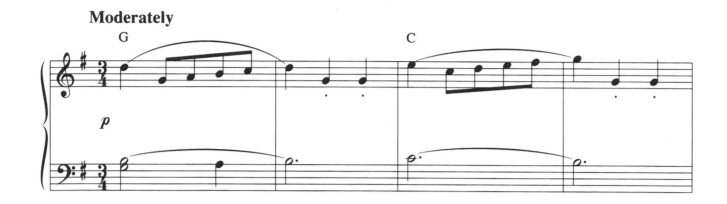

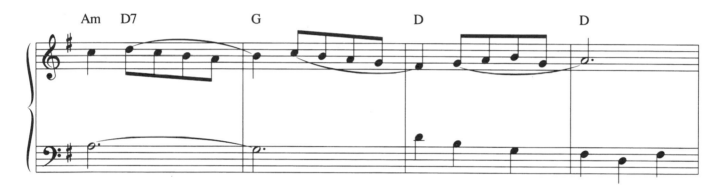

Musette In D

Music by Johann Sebastian Bach

Moderately

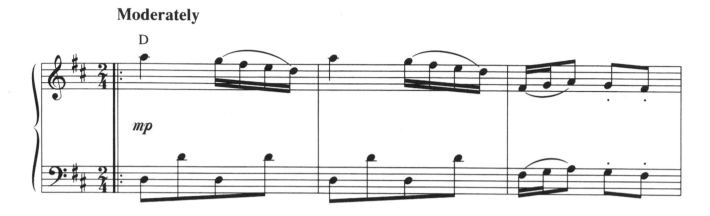

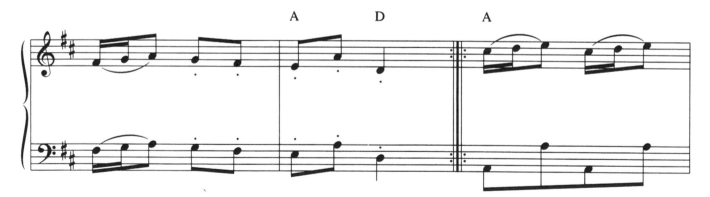

15

Passepied No. 1
(from *Orchestral Suite In C*)

Music by Johann Sebastian Bach

Bright

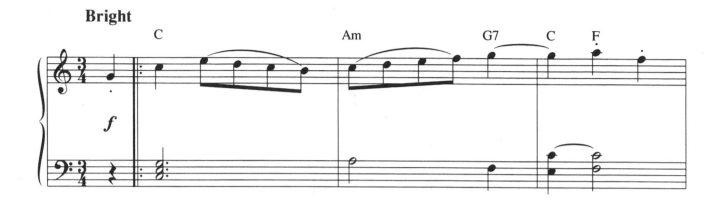

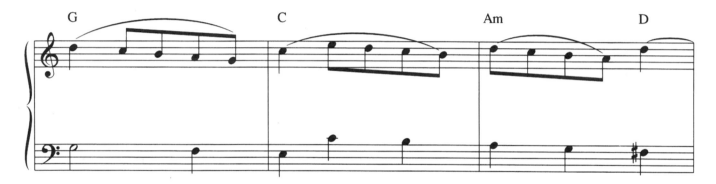

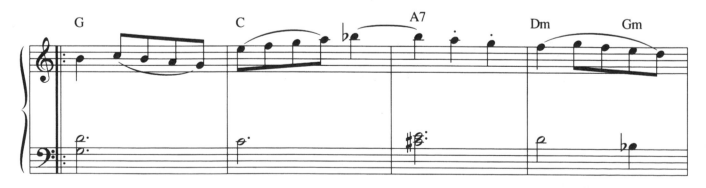

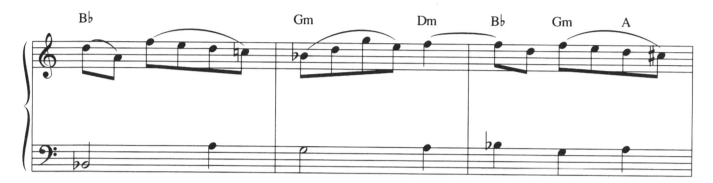

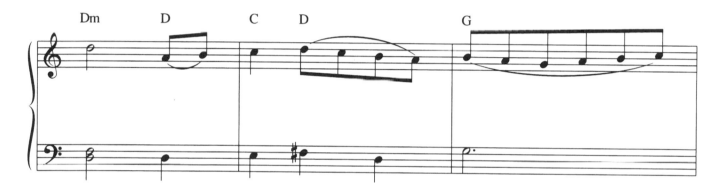

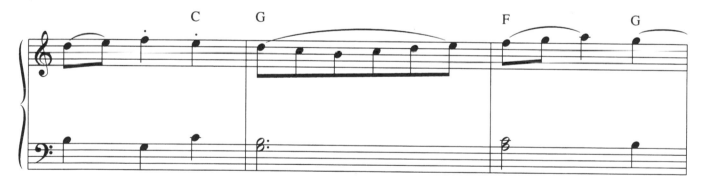

Sleepers, Wake!
A Voice Is Calling

Music by Johann Sebastian Bach

Moderately

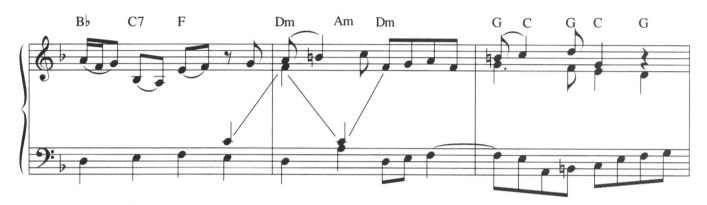

19

Themes
(from *Toccata And Fugue In D Minor*)

Music by Johann Sebastian Bach

Slow

Prelude In G Minor For Organ

Music by Johann Sebastian Bach

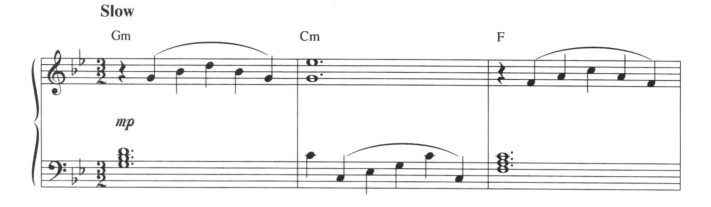

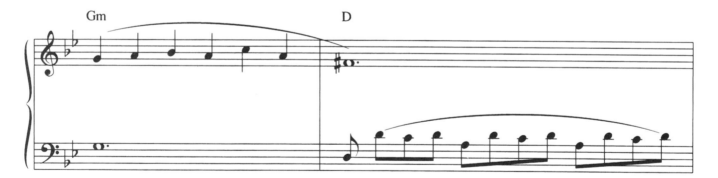

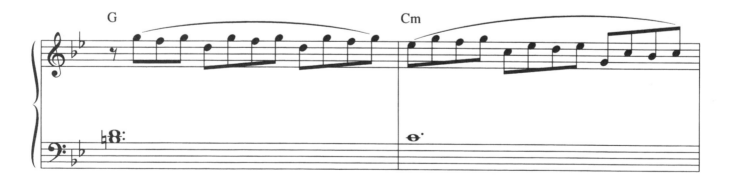

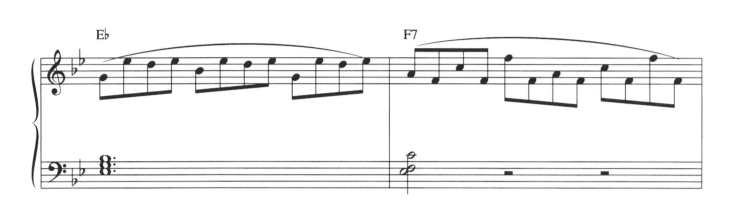

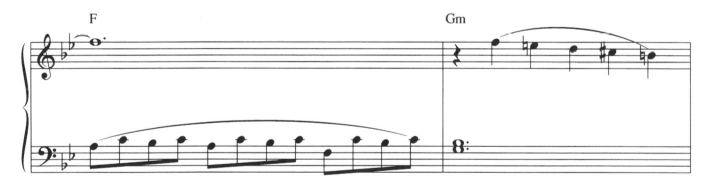

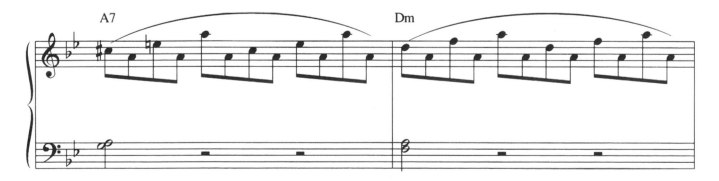

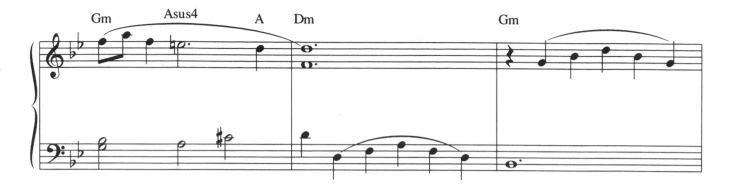

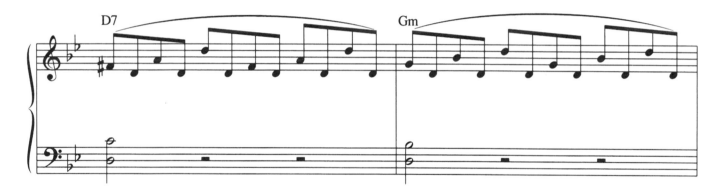

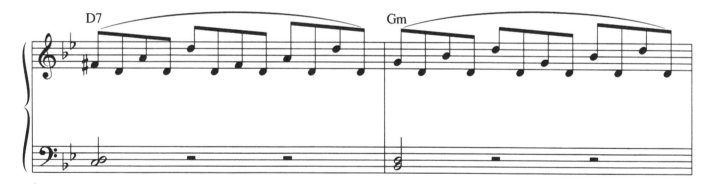

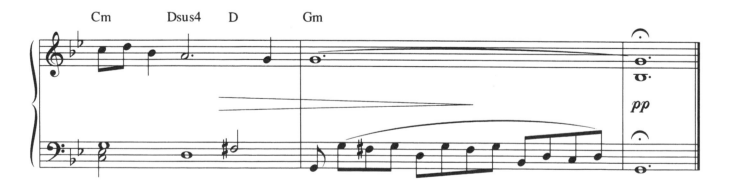

First Movement Themes

(from *Symphony No.5*)

Music by Ludwig Van Beethoven

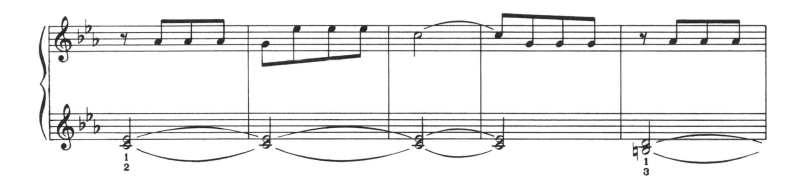

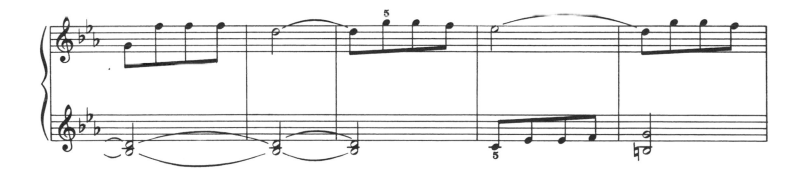

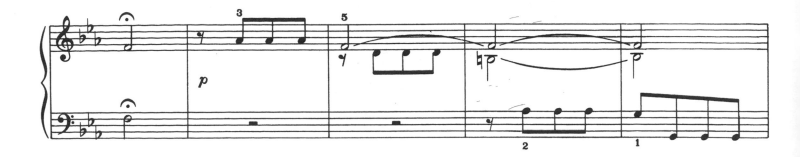

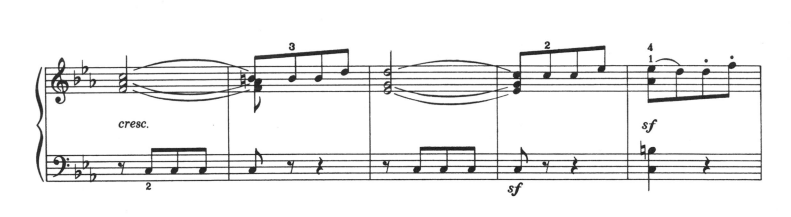

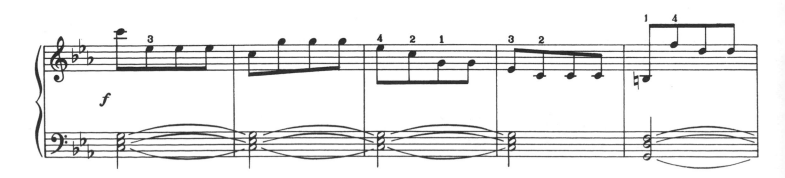

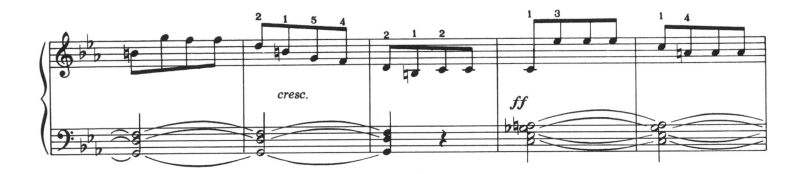

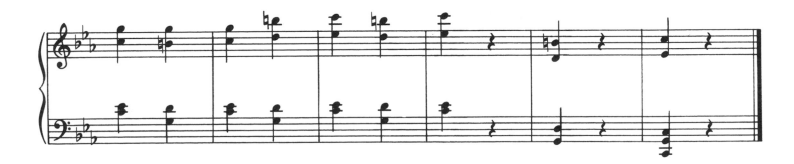

27

Für Elise

Music by Ludwig Van Beethoven

Not too fast

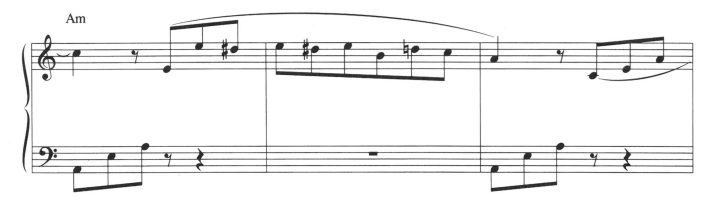

Minuet In G

Music by Ludwig Van Beethoven

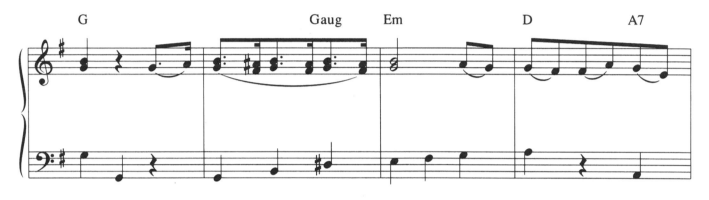

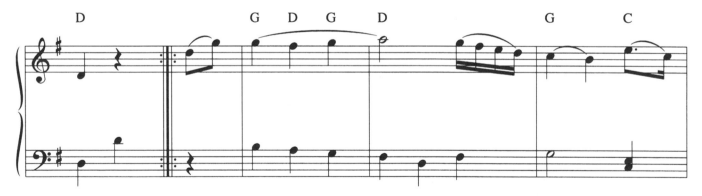

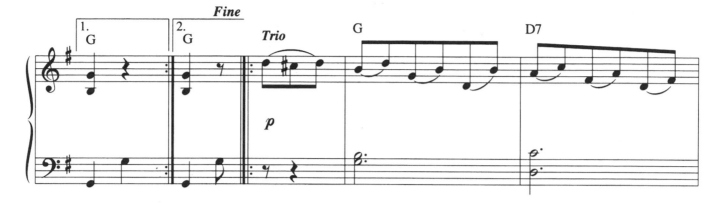

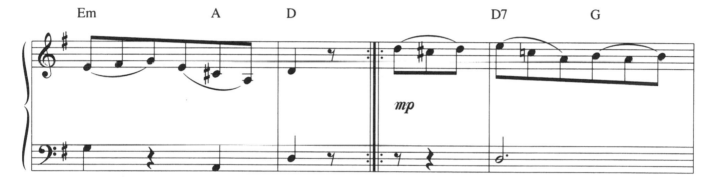

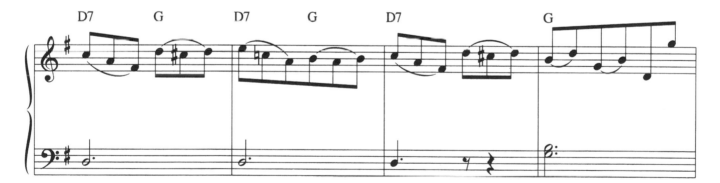

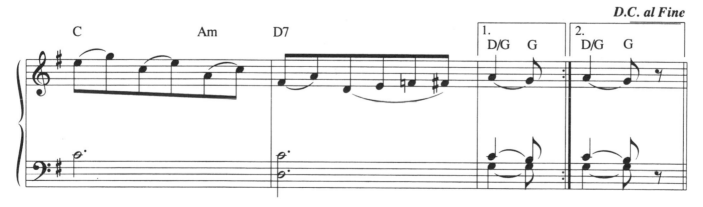

Ode To Joy
(from *The Choral Symphony*)

Music by Ludwig Van Beethoven

With movement

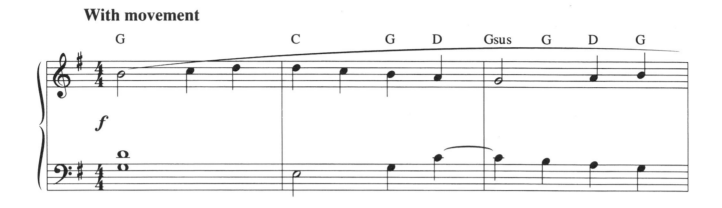

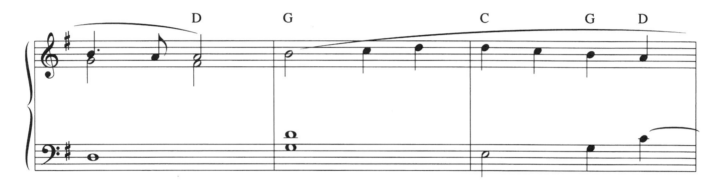

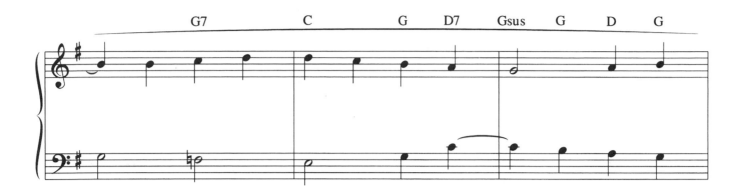

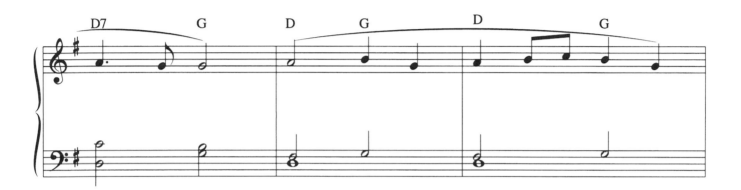

Slow Movement
(from *Sonata Pathétique*)

Music by Ludwig Van Beethoven

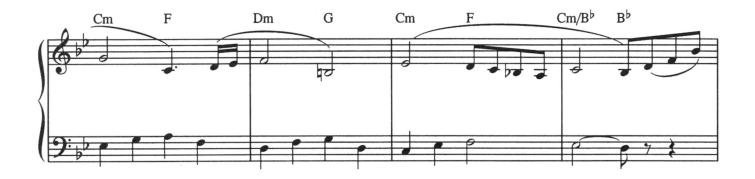

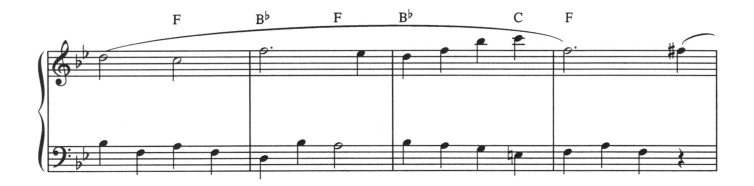

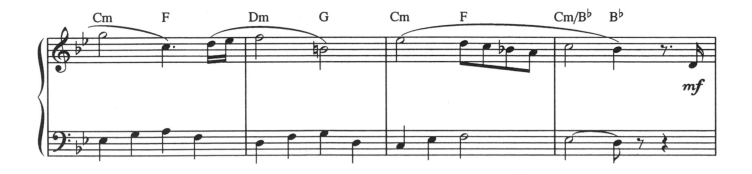

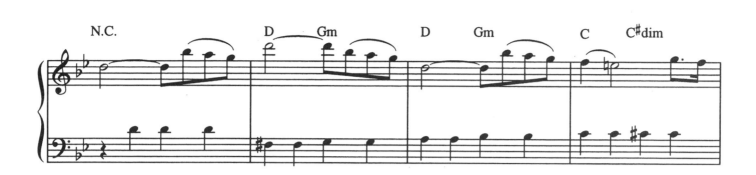

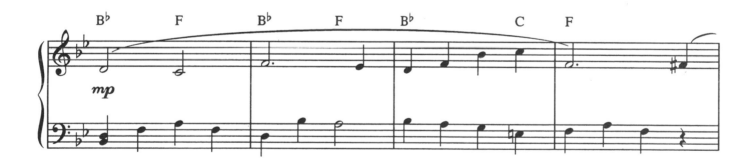

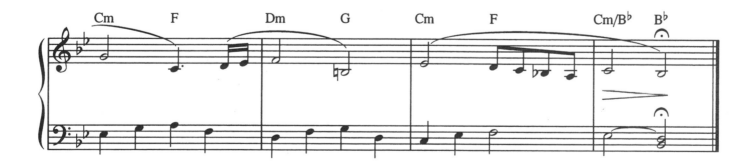

Theme

(from *The Eroica Symphony*)

Music by Ludwig Van Beethoven

Bright tempo

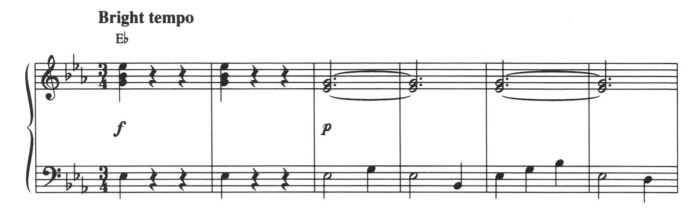

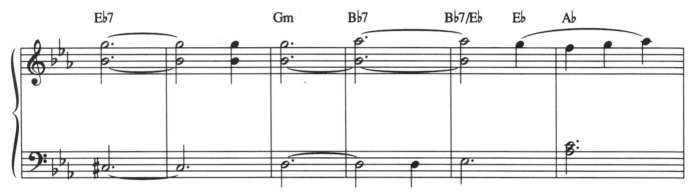

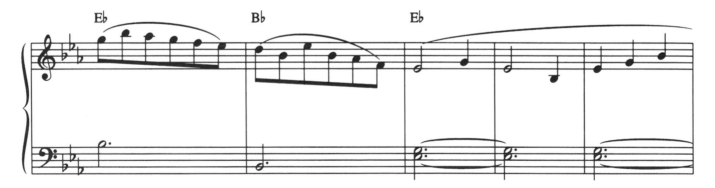

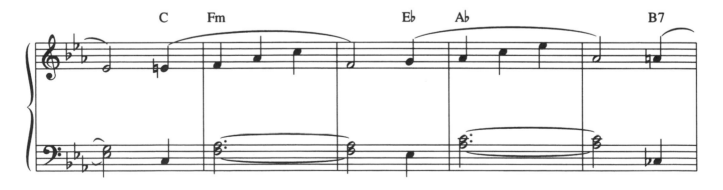

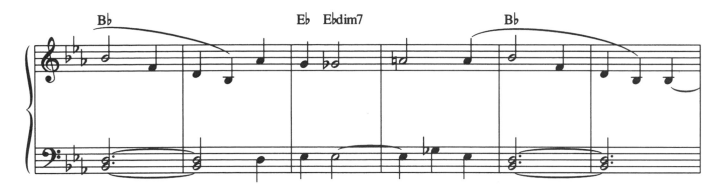

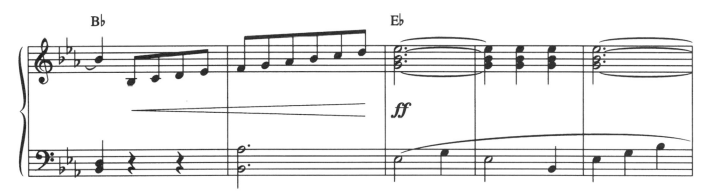

Theme

(from *The Pastoral Symphony*)

Music by Ludwig Van Beethoven

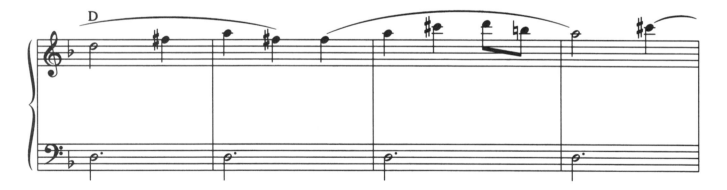

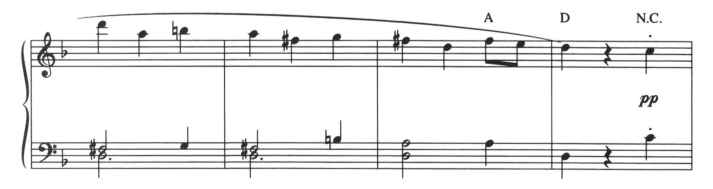

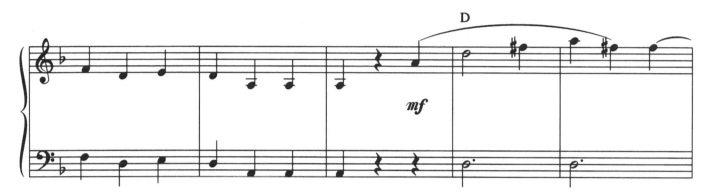

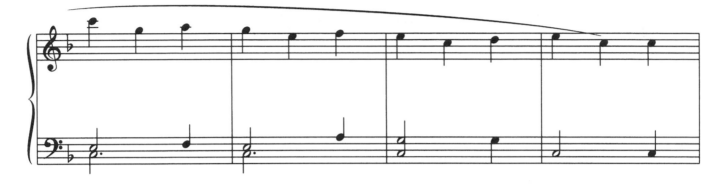

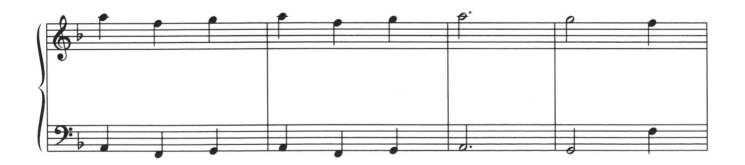

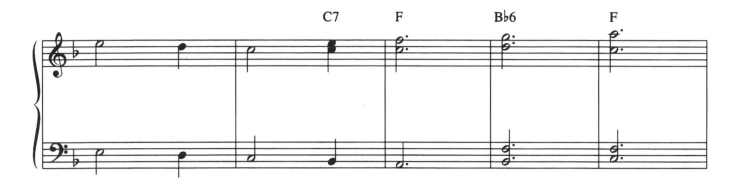

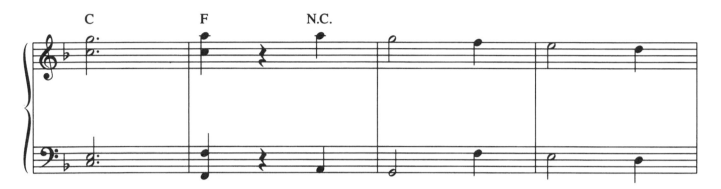

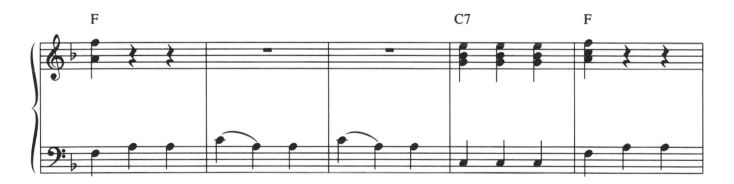

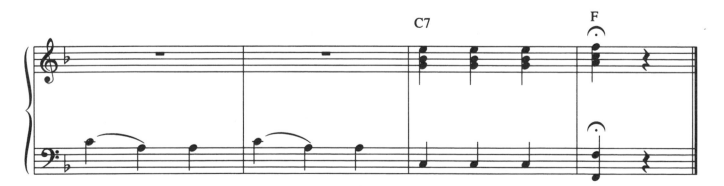

Theme
(from *Variations Op.26*)
Music by Ludwig Van Beethoven

Andante

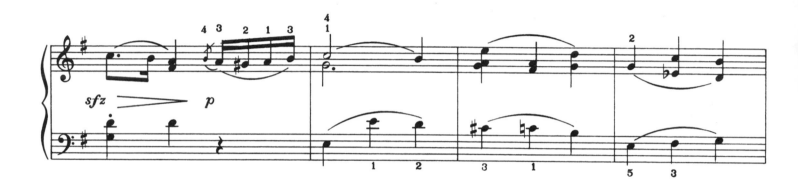

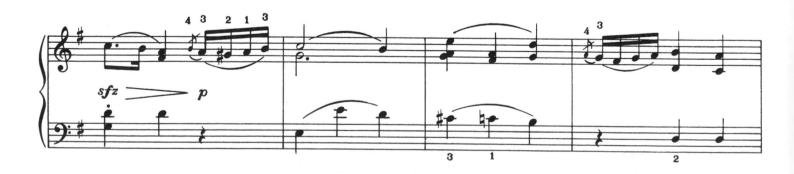

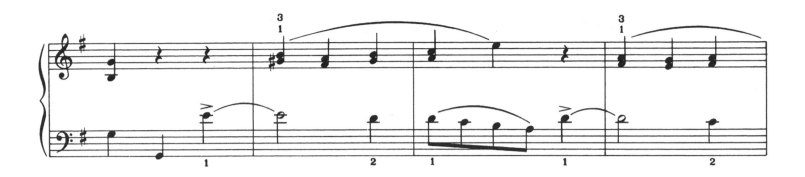

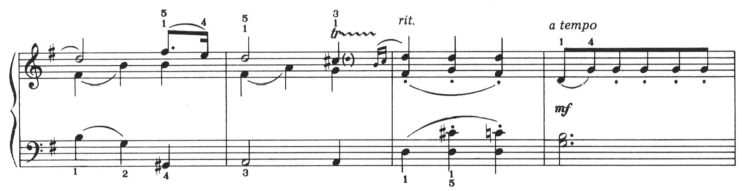

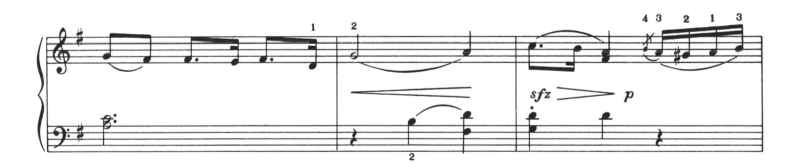

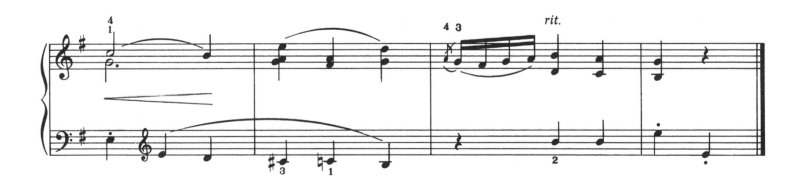

Slow Movement Theme
(from *Symphony No.5*)

Music by Ludwig Van Beethoven

Moderately

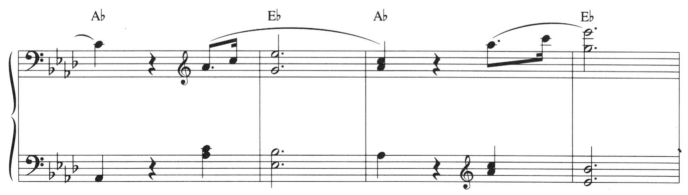

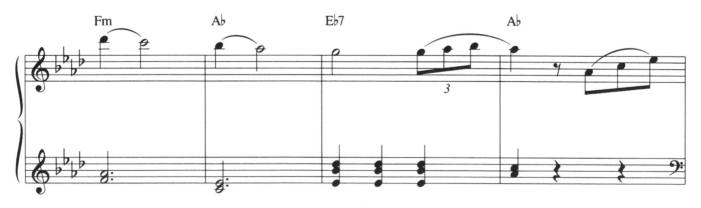

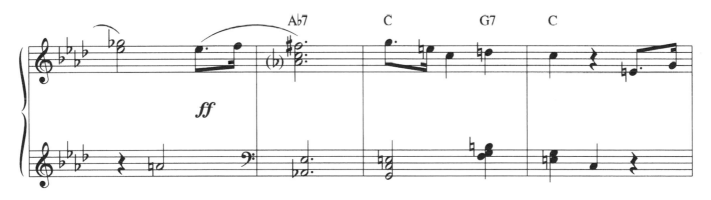

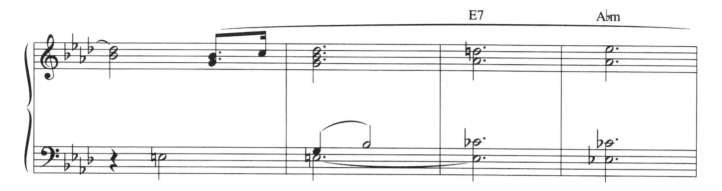

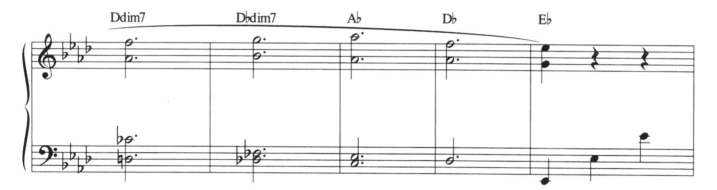

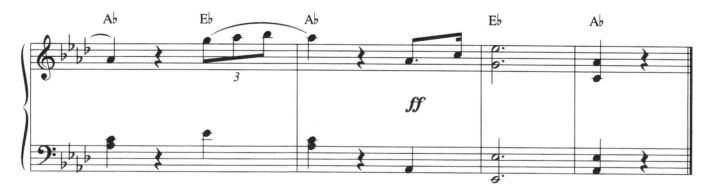

Duet
(from *The Pearl Fishers*)

Music by Georges Bizet

Moderately

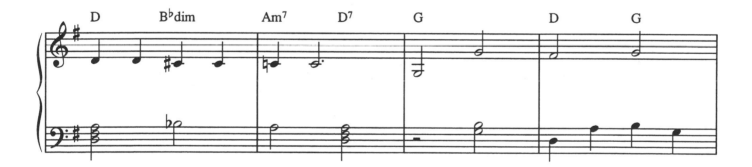

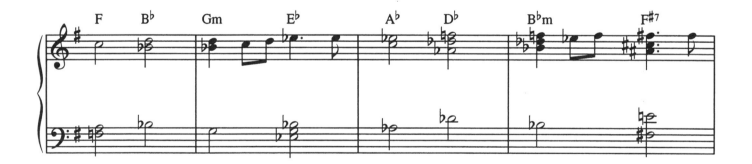

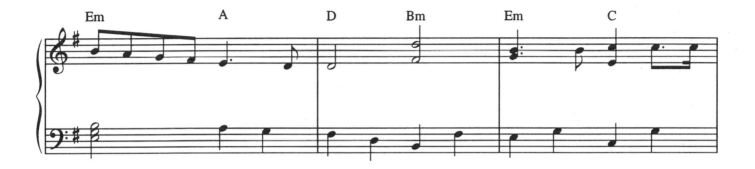

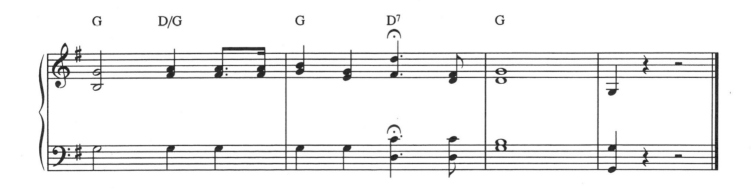

49

You Can't Evade The Truth

(from *Carmen*)

Words & Music by Georges Bizet

Slow

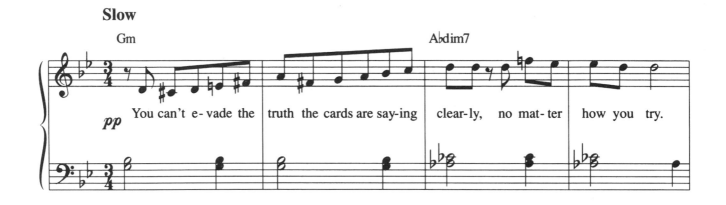

You can't e-vade the truth the cards are say-ing clear-ly, no mat-ter how you try.

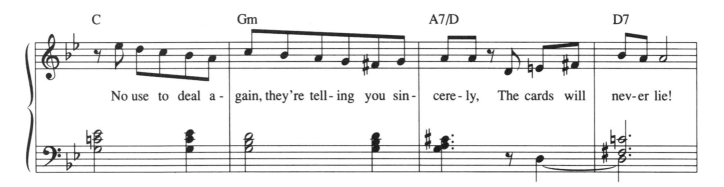

No use to deal a-gain, they're tell-ing you sin-cere-ly, The cards will nev-er lie!

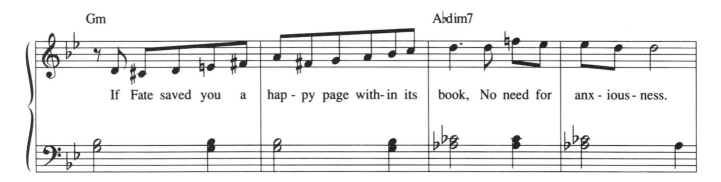

If Fate saved you a hap-py page with-in its book, No need for anx-ious-ness.

You know you'll get a luck-y card be-fore you look. Your fate is hap-pi-ness.

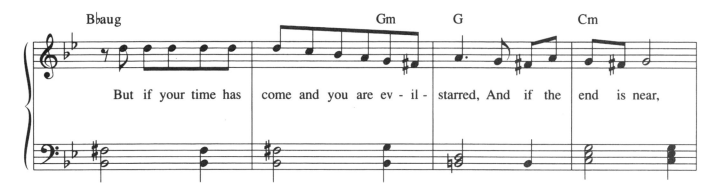

But if your time has come and you are ev-il-starred, And if the end is near,

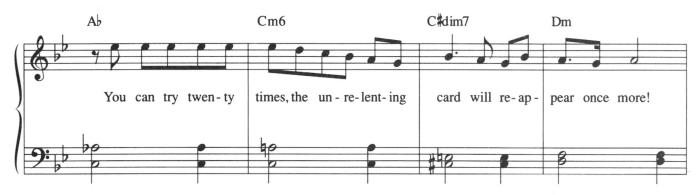

You can try twen-ty times, the un-re-lent-ing card will re-ap-pear once more!

If you are ev-il-starred and there is death in store,___ The un-re-lent-ing

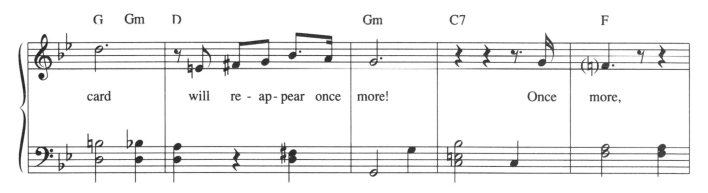

card will re-ap-pear once more! Once more,

Once more, There's death in store.___

Minuet
(from *String Quartet*)

Music by Luigi Boccherini

Moderately

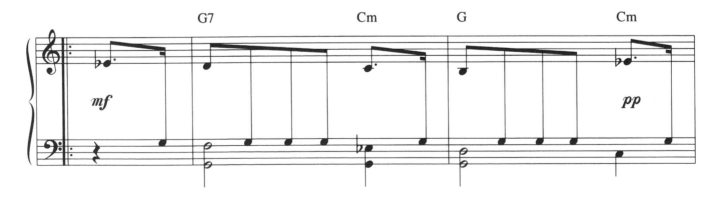

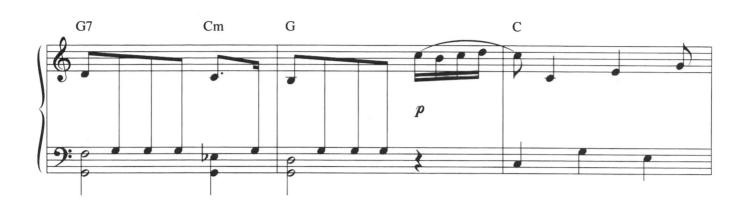

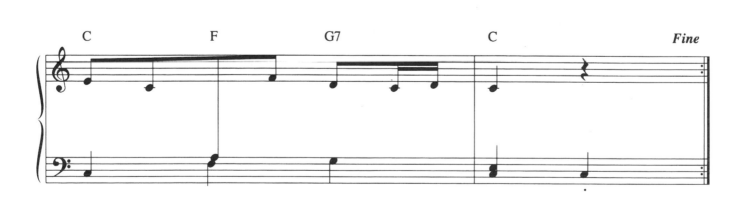

Theme

(from *Variations On A Theme By Haydn*)

Music by Johannes Brahms

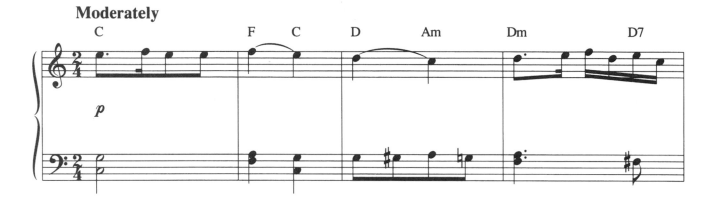

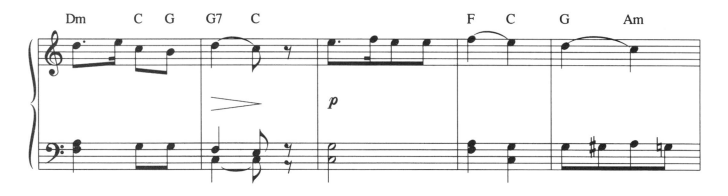

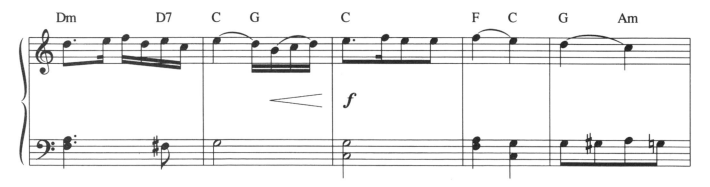

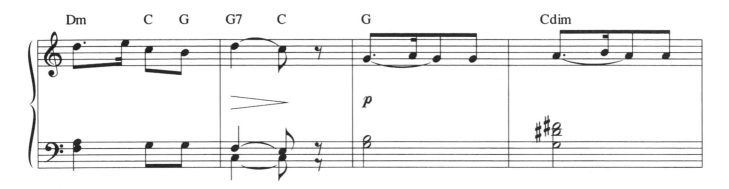

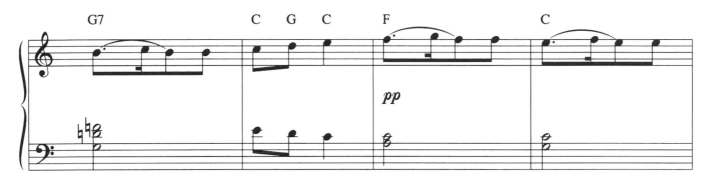

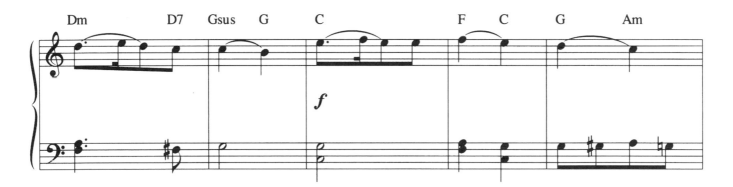

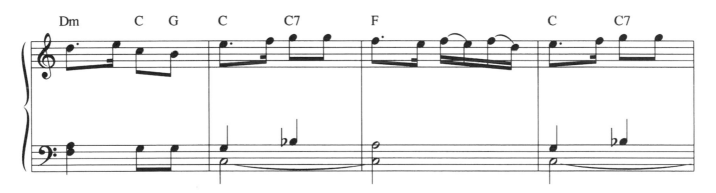

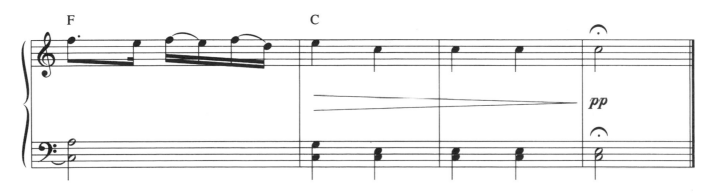

Flower Duet
(from *Lakmé*)

Music by Leo Delibes

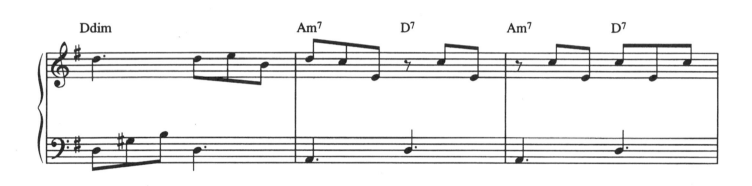

Largo
(from *The New World Symphony*)

Music by Antonín Dvořák

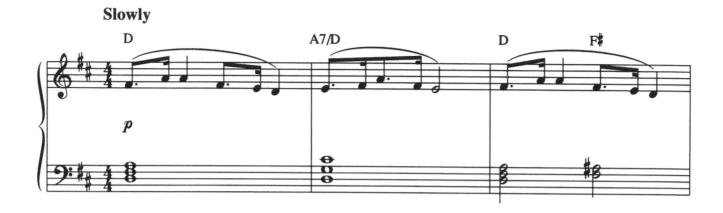

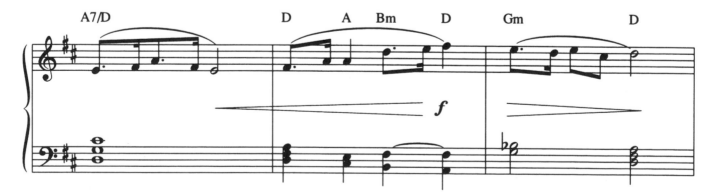

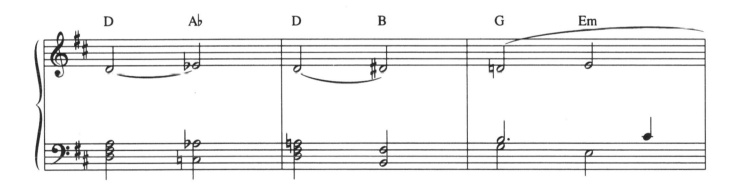

Nimrod
(from *The Enigma Variations*)

Music by Edward Elgar

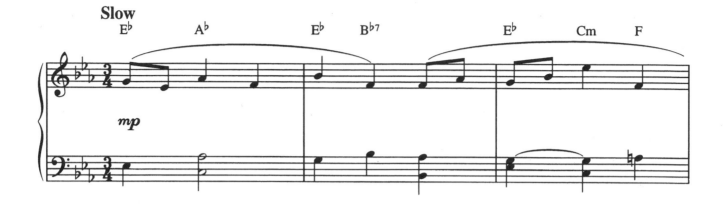

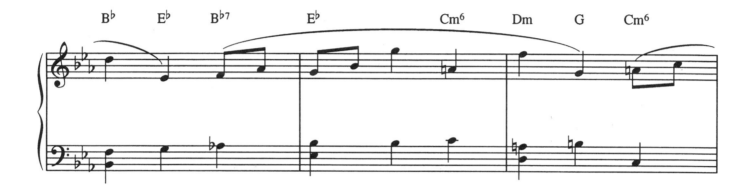

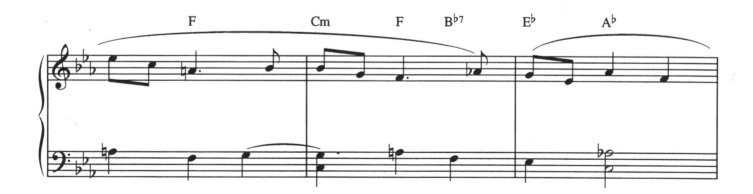

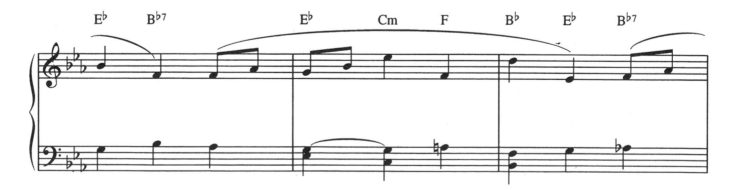

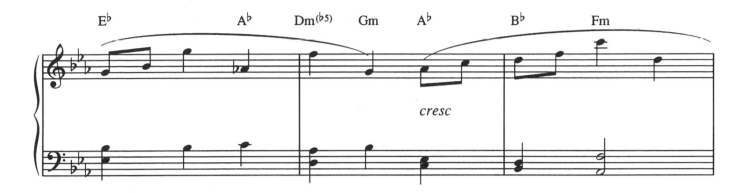

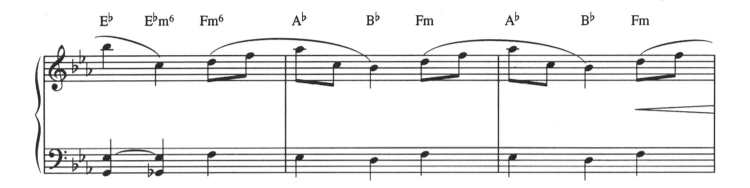

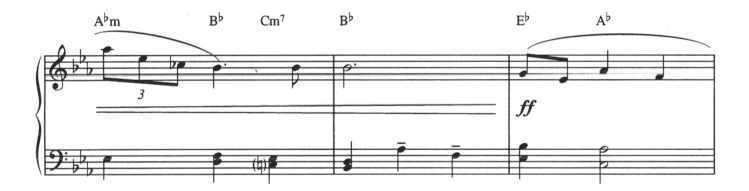

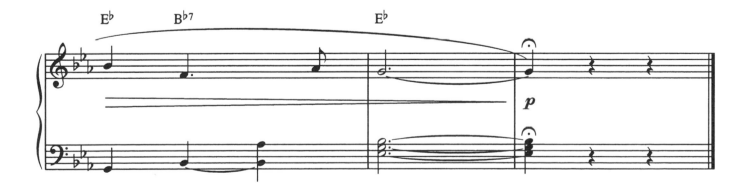

Oh! Wake Not Yet

(from *Jocelyn*)

Words & Music by Benjamin Godard

Moderately

Oh! Wake not yet our dream,

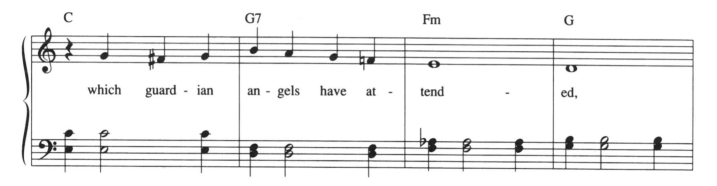

which guard - ian an - gels have at - tend - ed,

And while the gold - en splen - dours gleam, Still

sleep, my love, un - til 'tis

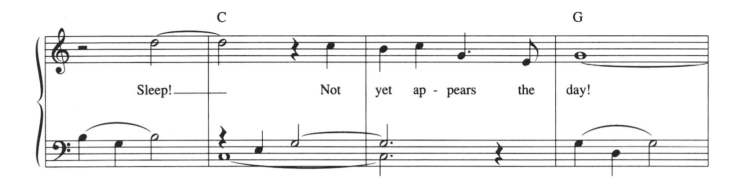

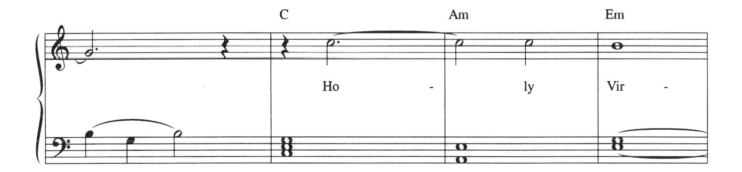

Trumpet Voluntary

Music by Jeremiah Clarke

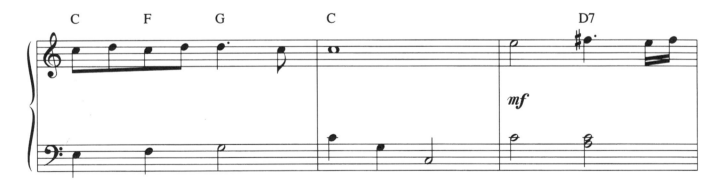

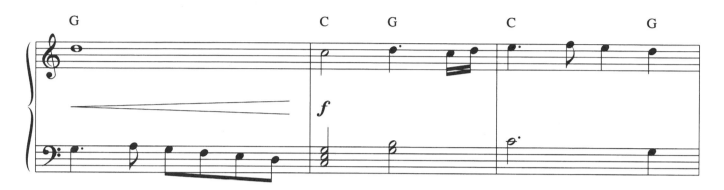

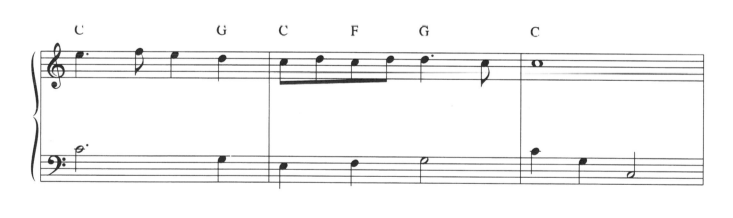

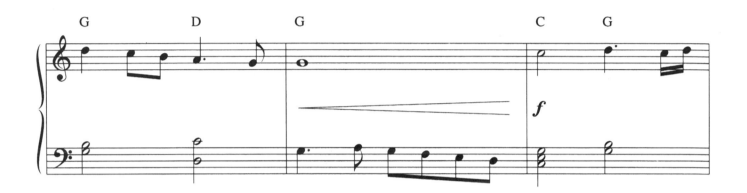

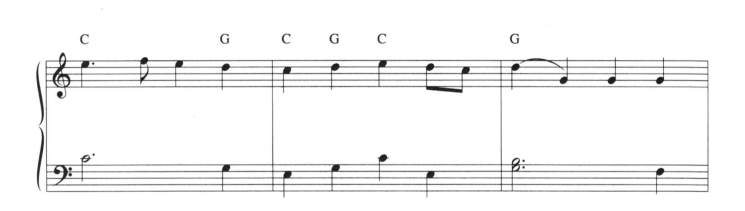

Morning
(from *The Peer Gynt Suite*)

Music by Edvard Grieg

Not too fast

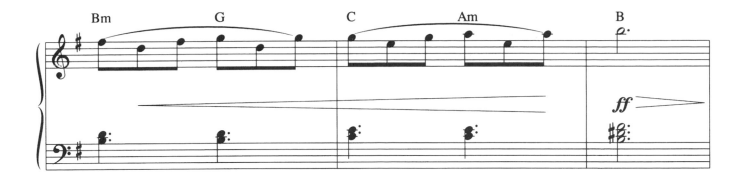

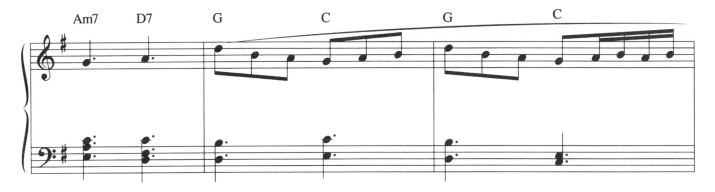

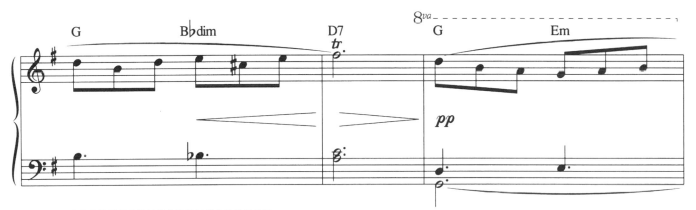

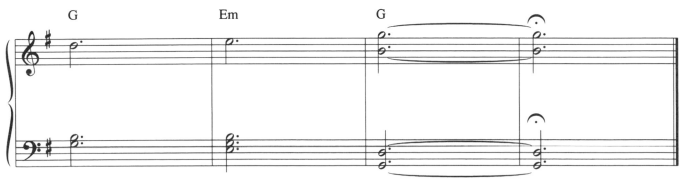

Slow Movement
(from *Piano Concerto In G Minor*)

Music by Edvard Grieg

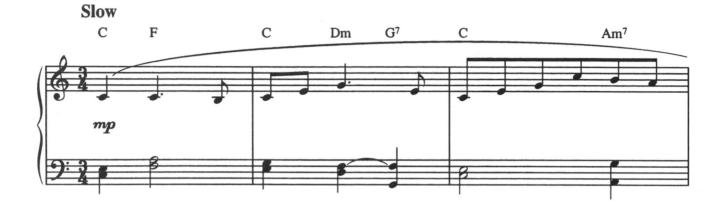

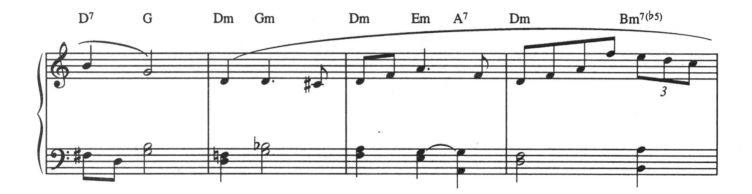

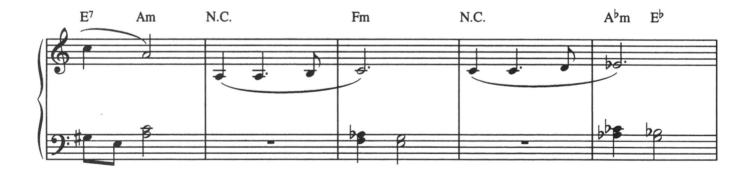

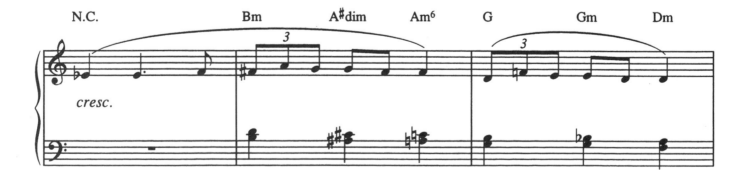

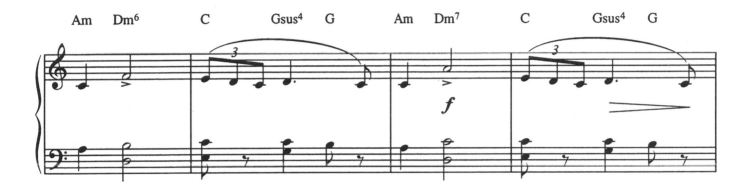

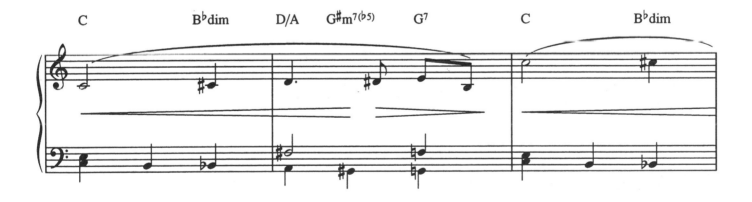

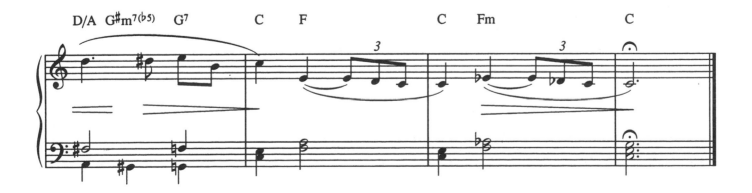

Hallelujah Chorus
(from *Messiah*)

Music by George Frideric Handel

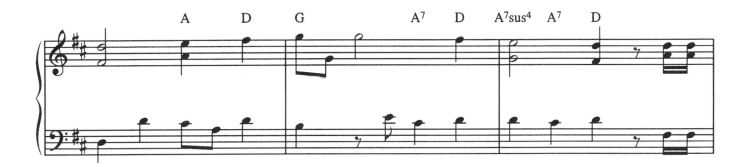

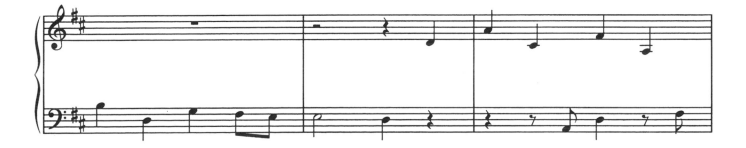

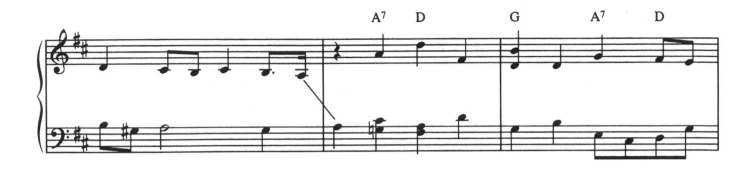

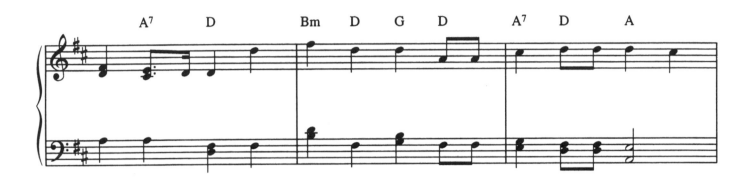

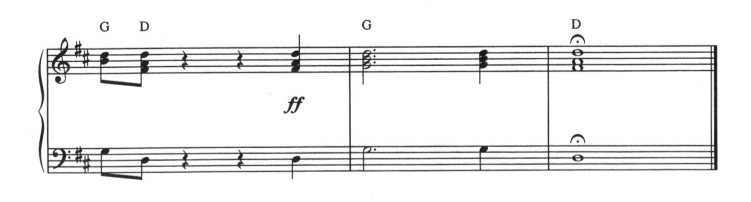

Largo
(from *Xerxes*)

Music by George Frideric Handel

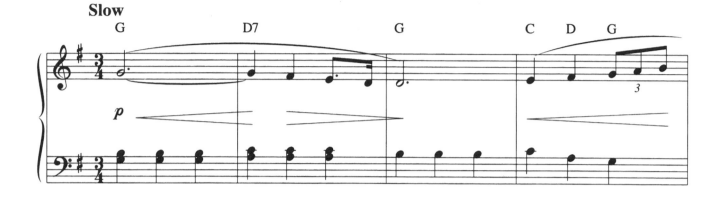

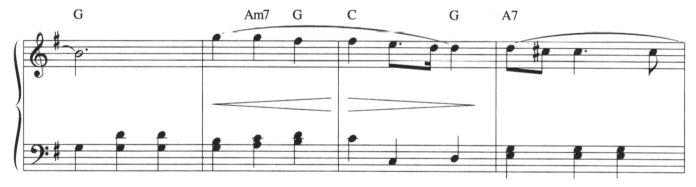

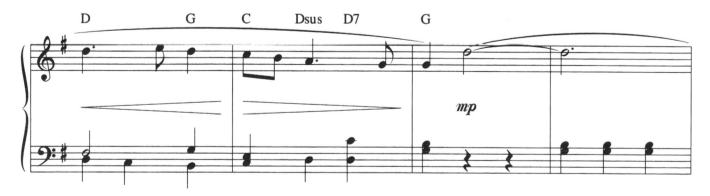

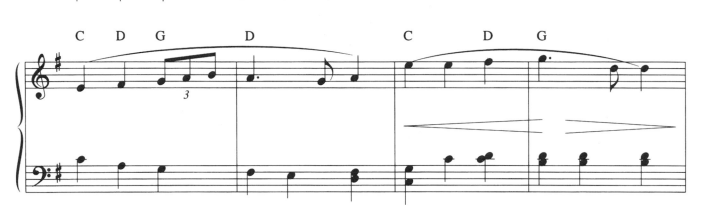

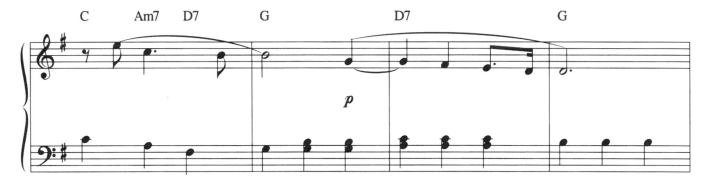

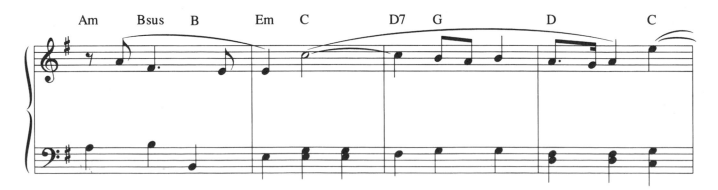

76

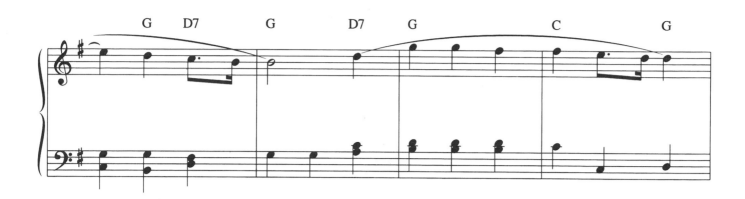

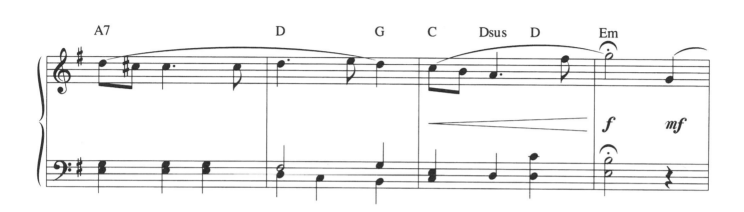

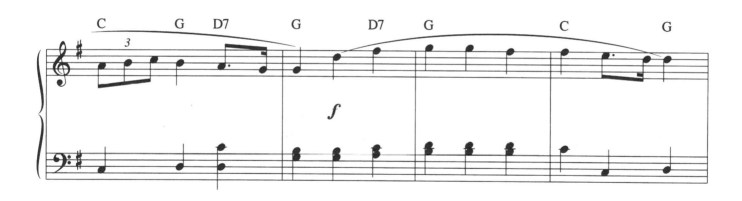

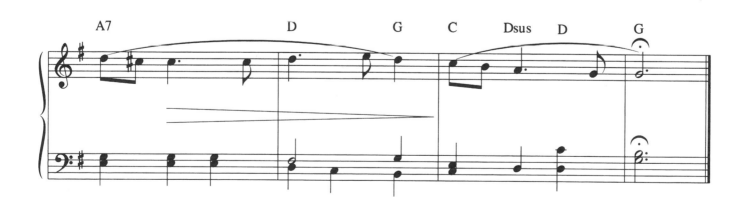

Theme
(from *The London Symphony*)

Music by Franz Josef Haydn

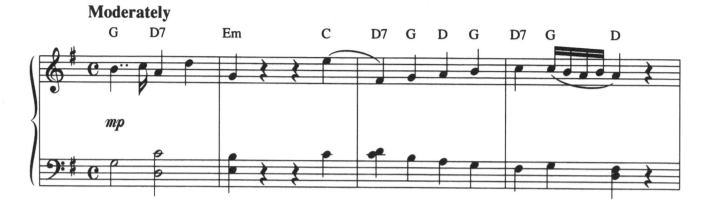

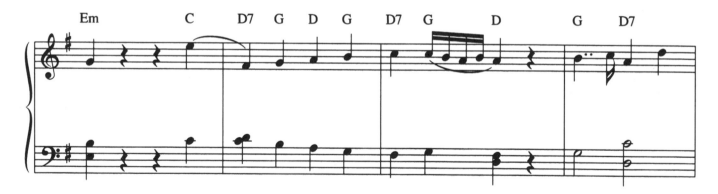

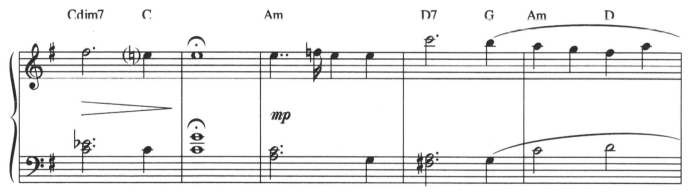

79

Theme

(from *The Surprise Symphony*)

Music by Franz Josef Haydn

Moderately

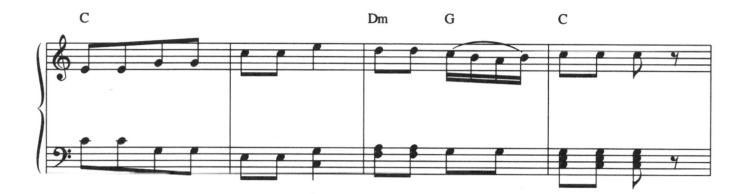

O, For The Wings Of A Dove

Music by Felix Mendelssohn

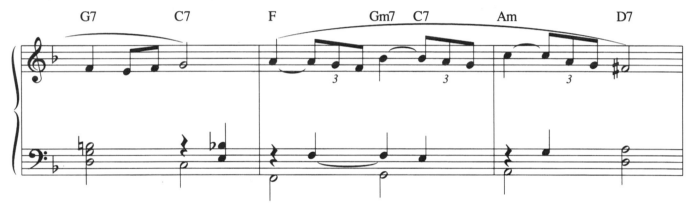

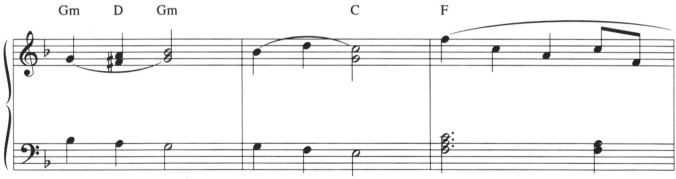

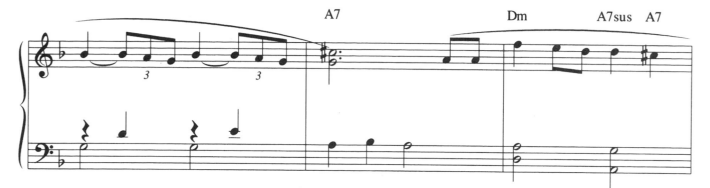

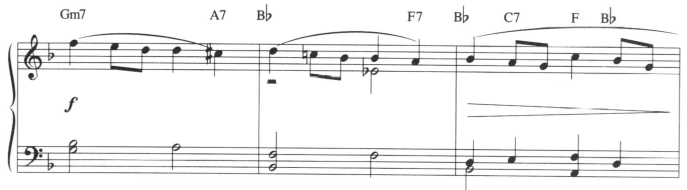

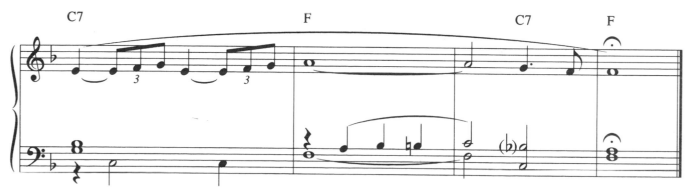

On Wings Of Song

Music by Felix Mendelssohn

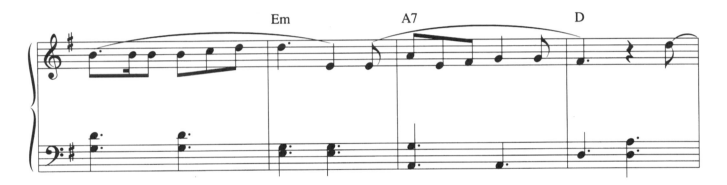

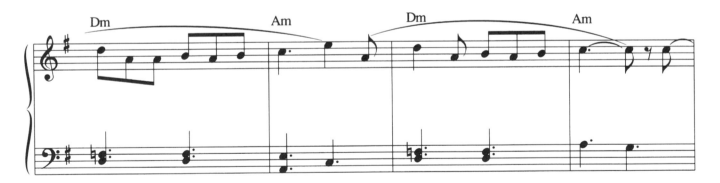

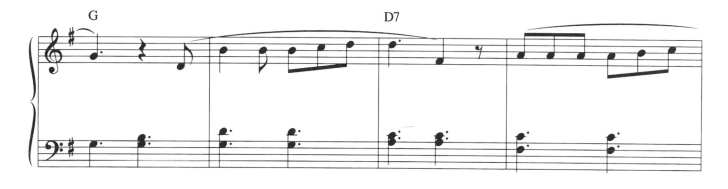

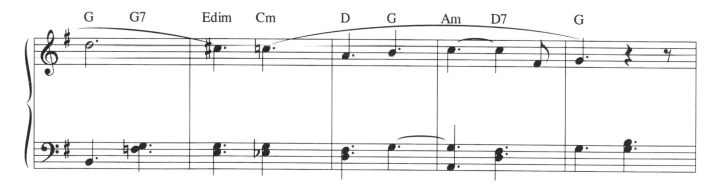

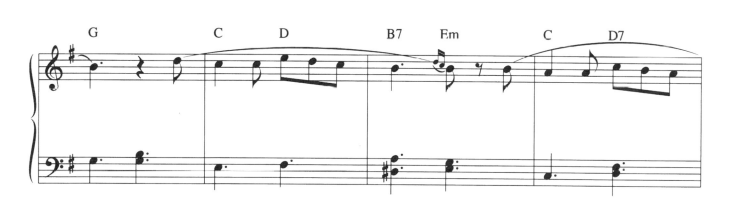

Theme

(from *The Scottish Symphony*)

Music by Felix Mendelssohn

Moderately slow

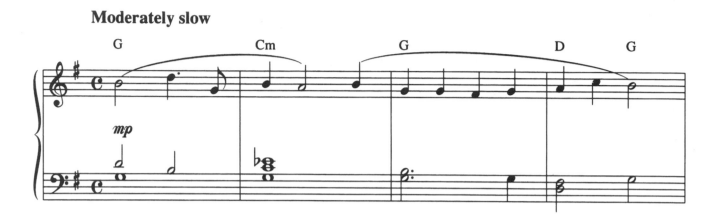

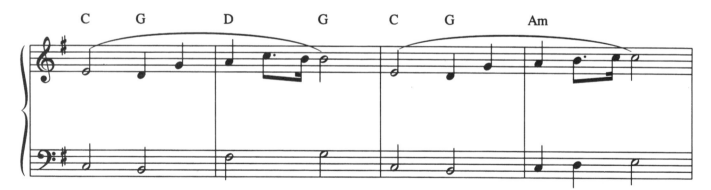

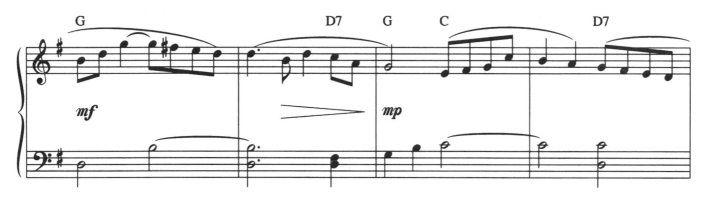

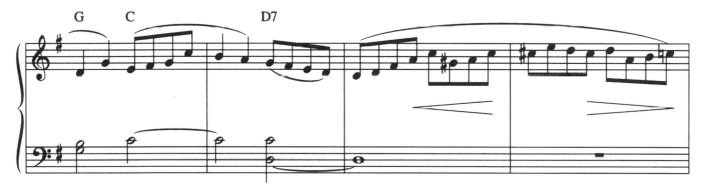

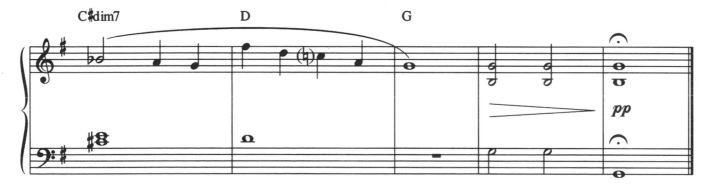

Wedding March
(from *A Midsummer Night's Dream*)

Music by Felix Mendelssohn

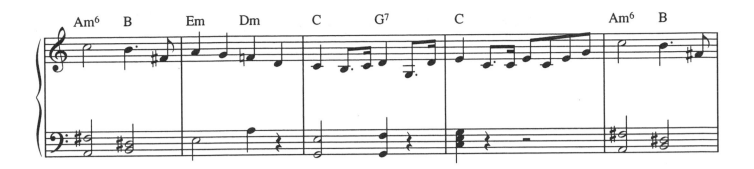

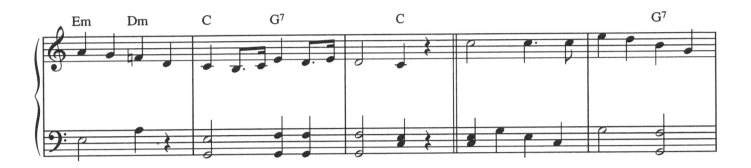

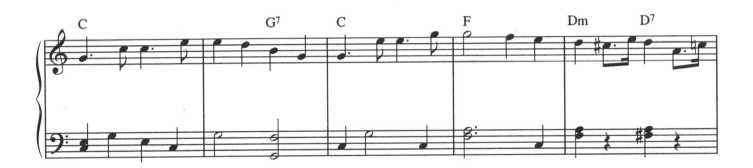

Ave Verum Corpus In D

Music by Wolfgang Amadeus Mozart

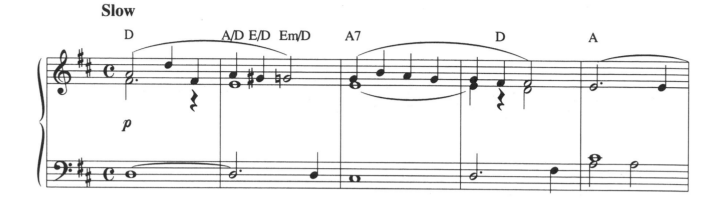

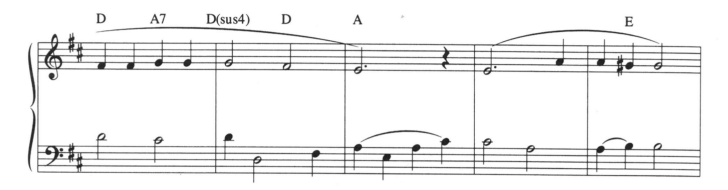

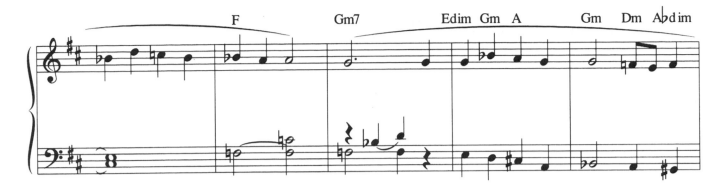

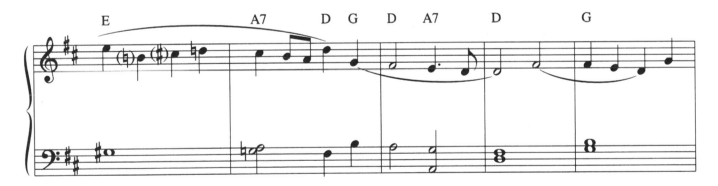

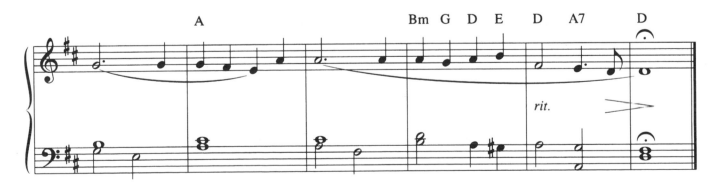

First Movement Theme

(from *Eine Kleine Nachtmusik*)

Music by Wolfgang Amadeus Mozart

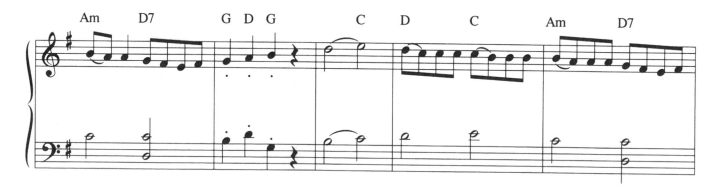

93

Romance
(from *Eine Kleine Nachtmusik*)

Music by Wolfgang Amadeus Mozart

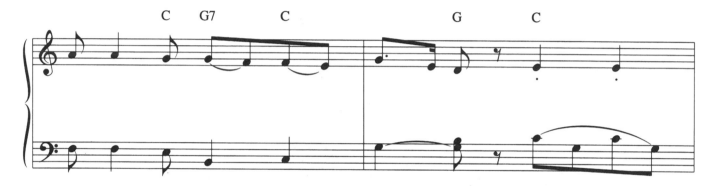

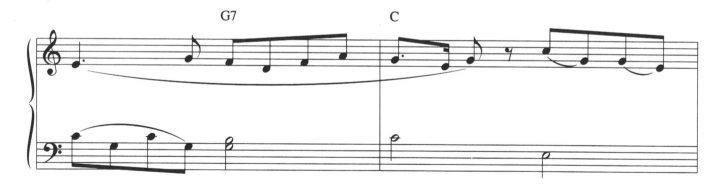

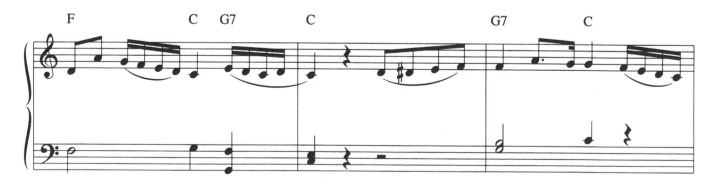

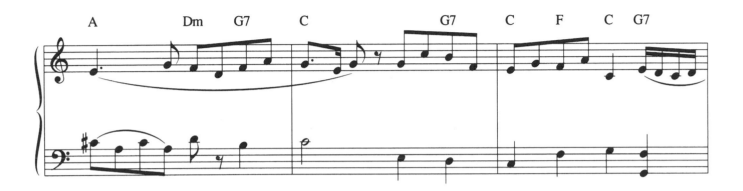

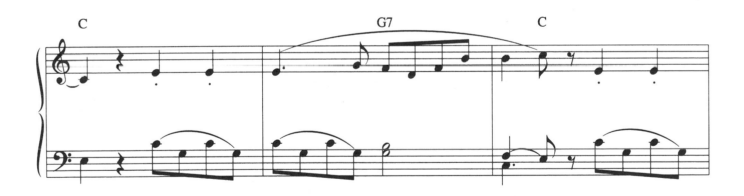

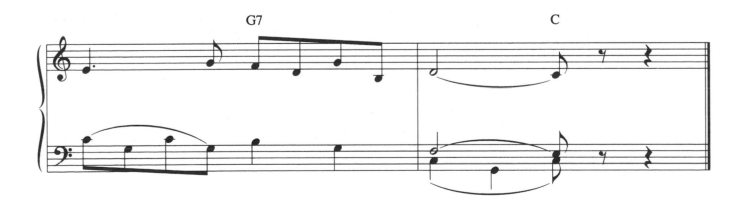

March Of The Priests

(from *The Magic Flute*)

Music by Wolfgang Amadeus Mozart

Moderately

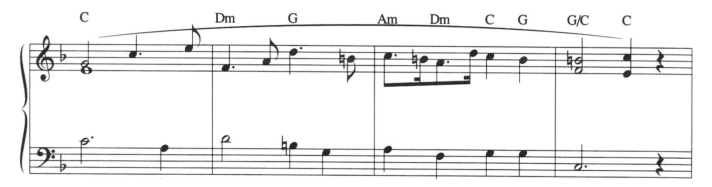

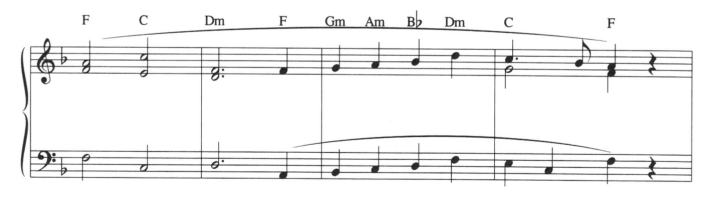

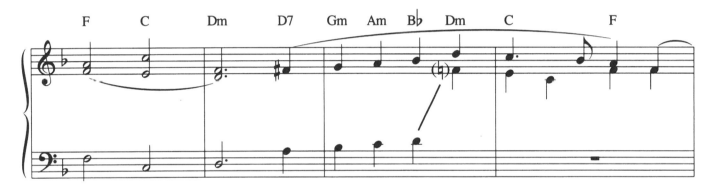

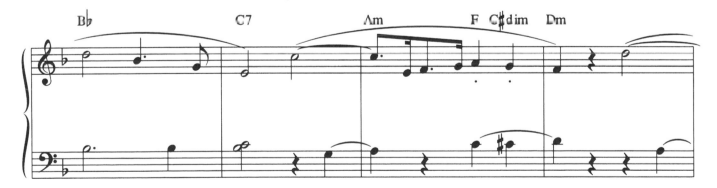

Minuet In F

Music by Wolfgang Amadeus Mozart

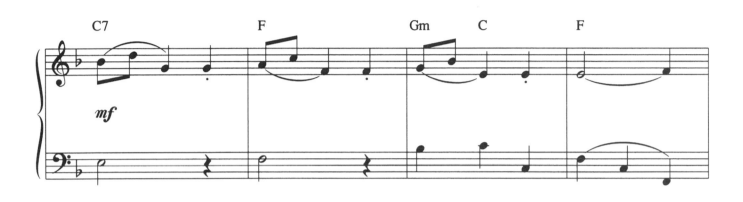

99

Piano Concerto No.21 In C
(Theme from *Elvira Madigan*)

Music by Wolfgang Amadeus Mozart

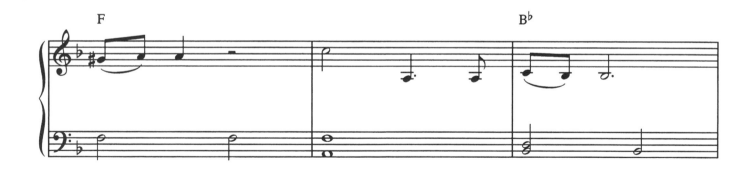

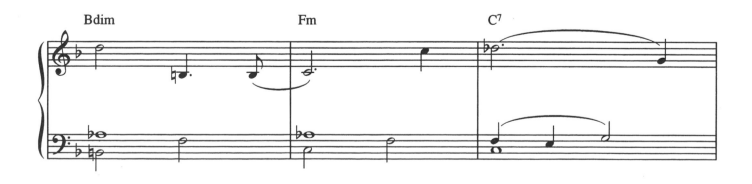

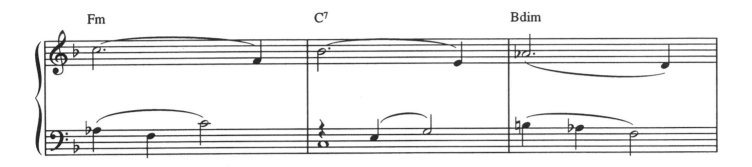

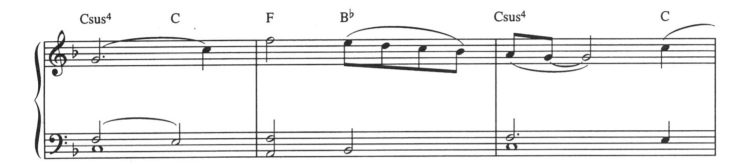

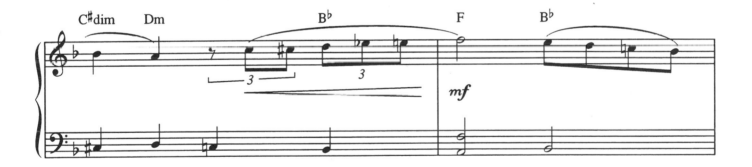

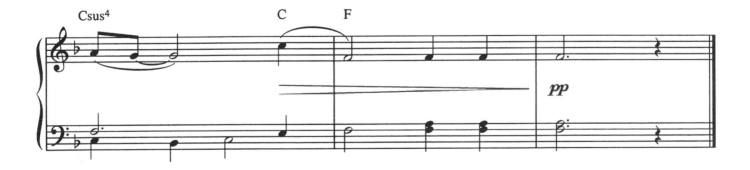

Non Più Andrai
(from *The Marriage Of Figaro*)

Music by Wolfgang Amadeus Mozart

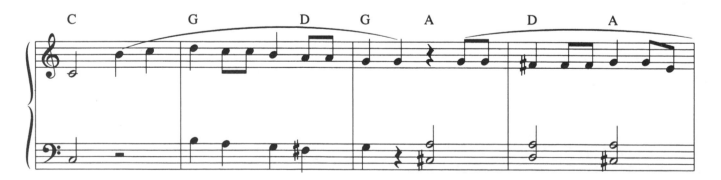

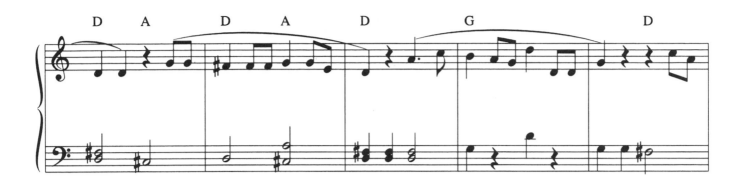

Theme
(from *Symphony In G Minor*)
Music by Wolfgang Amadeus Mozart

With movement

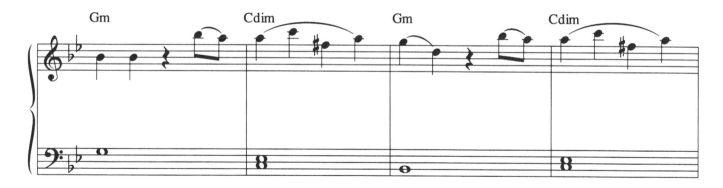

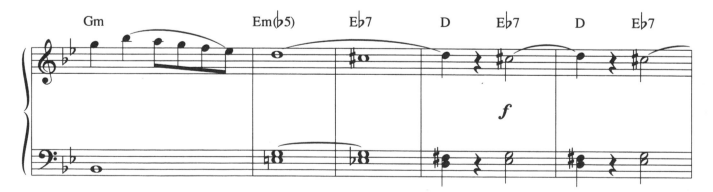

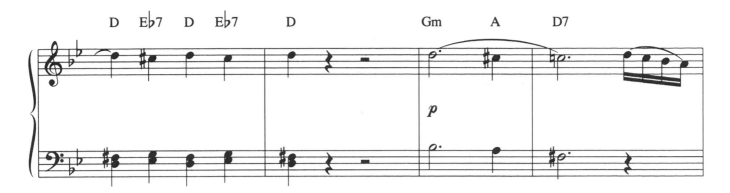

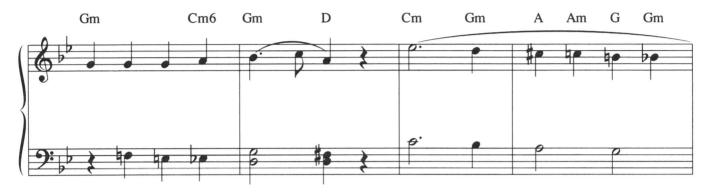

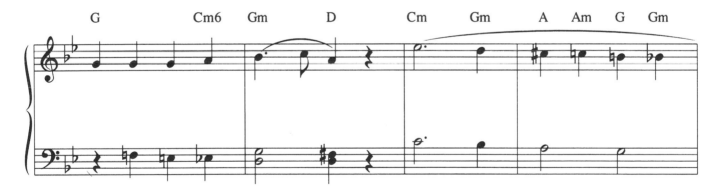

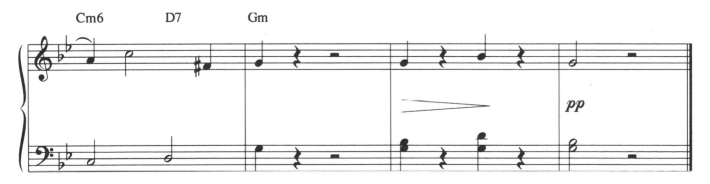

Minuet And Trio
(from *Symphony In F*)
Music by Wolfgang Amadeus Mozart

Moderately

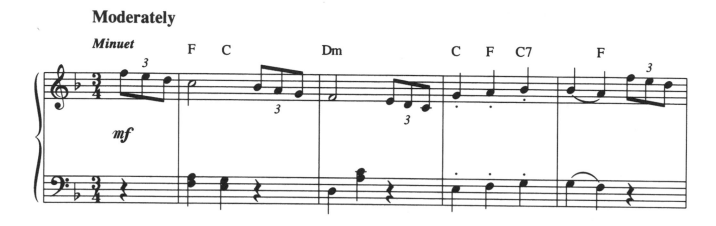

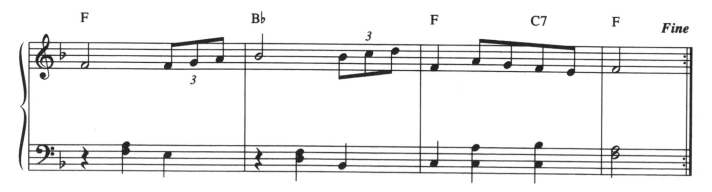

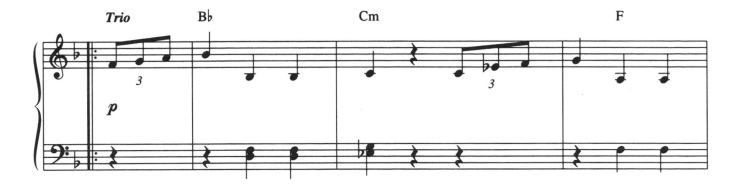

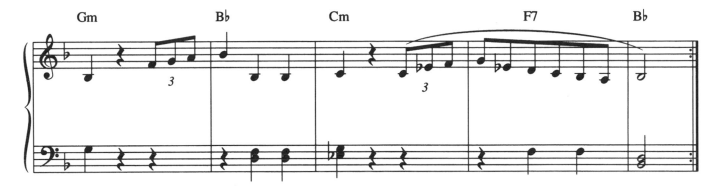

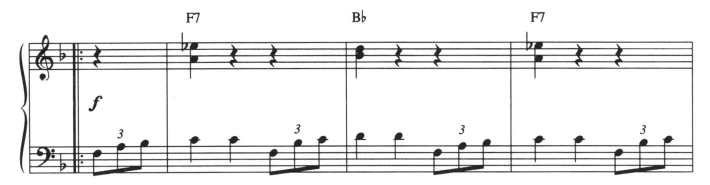

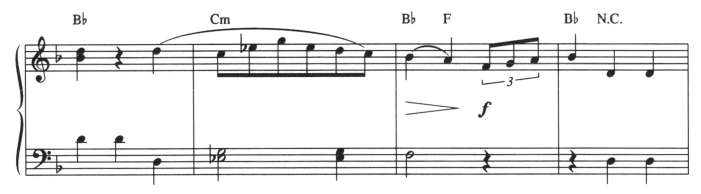

D.C. Minuet

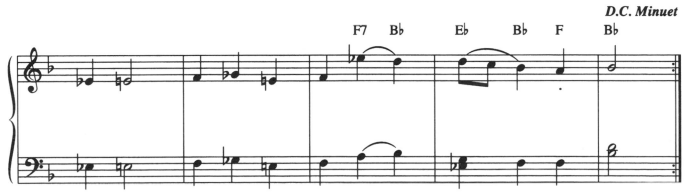

La Ci Darem La Mano
(from *Don Giovanni*)

Music by Wolfgang Amadeus Mozart

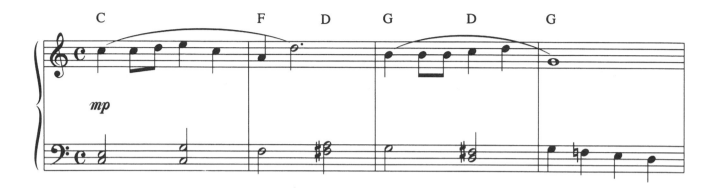

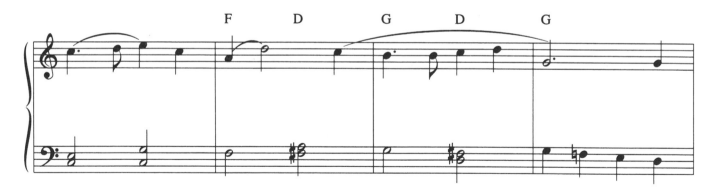

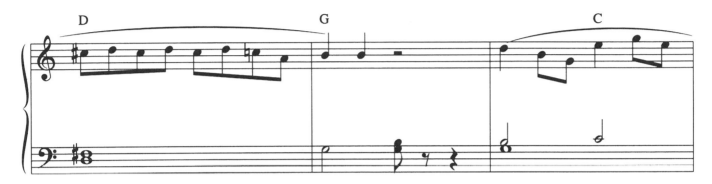

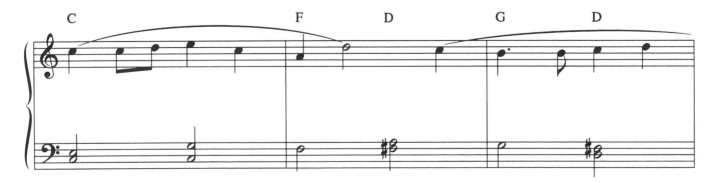

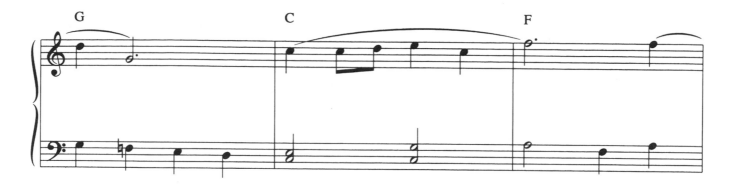

110

Dance Of The Hours
(from *La Gioconda*)

Music by Amilcare Ponchielli

Moderately

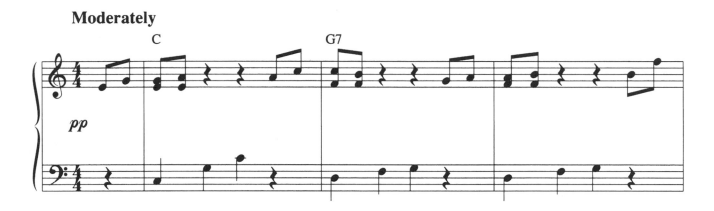

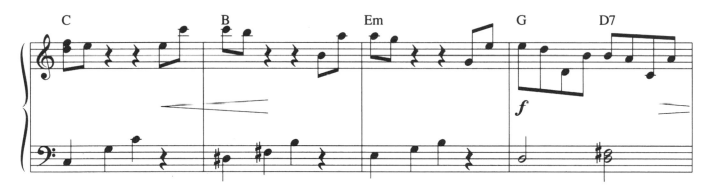

Canon In D

Music by Johann Pachelbel

Moderately

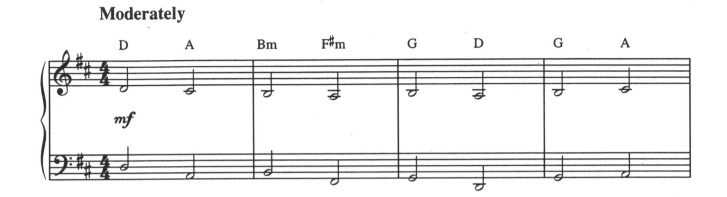

Rondo In D Minor
(from *Abdelazer*)

Music by Henry Purcell

Moderately

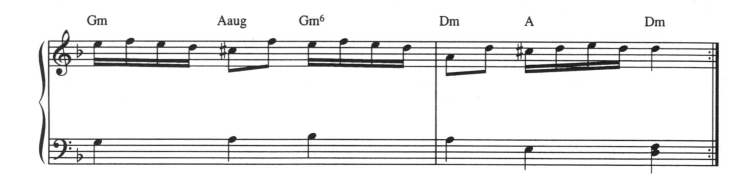

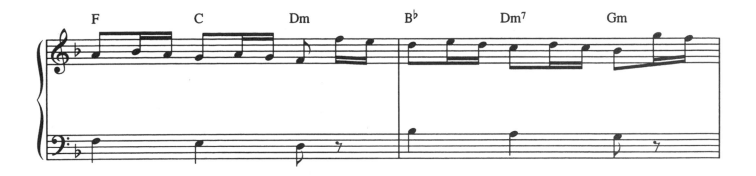

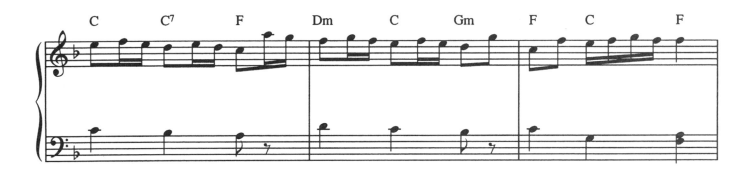

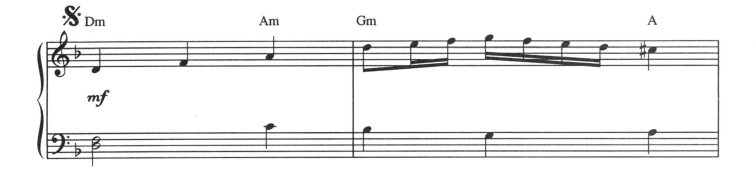

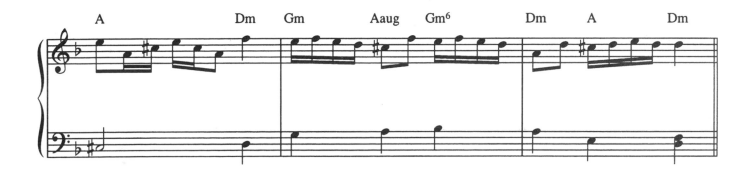

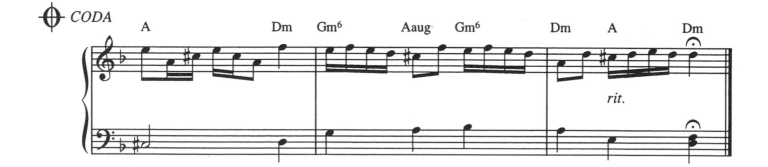

Trumpet Tune

Music by Henry Purcell

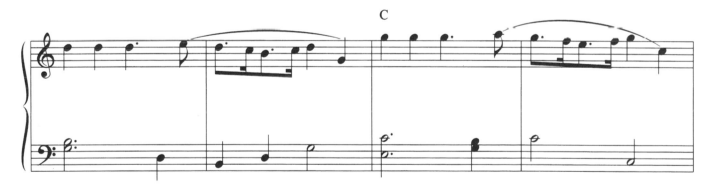

When I Am Laid In Earth

(from *Dido and Aeneas*)

Words & Music by Henry Purcell

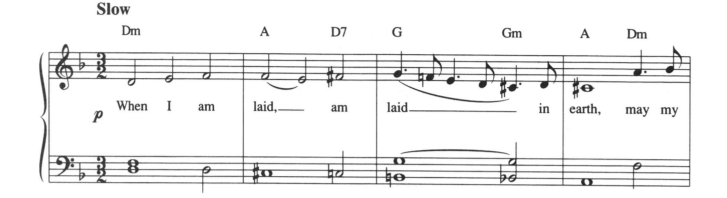

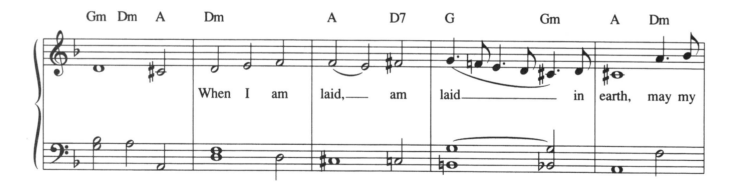

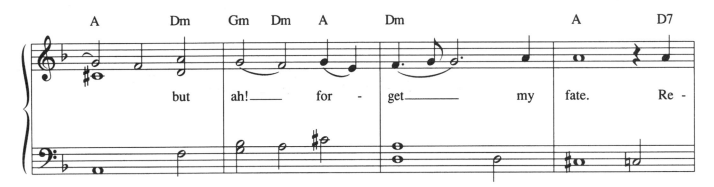

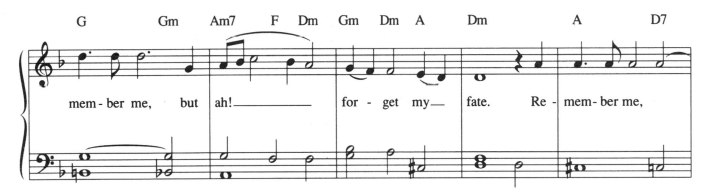

Impromptu Op.142 No.3

Music by Franz Schubert

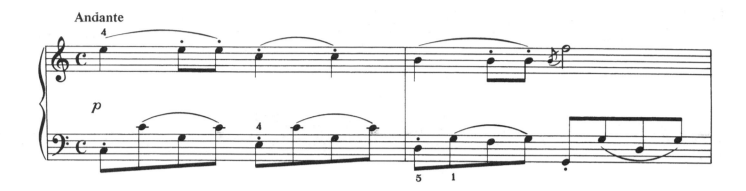

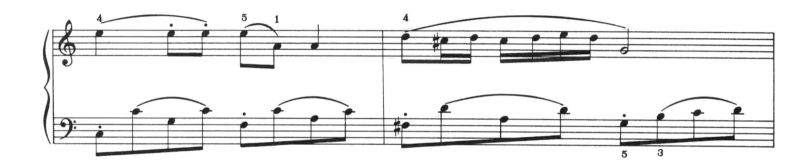

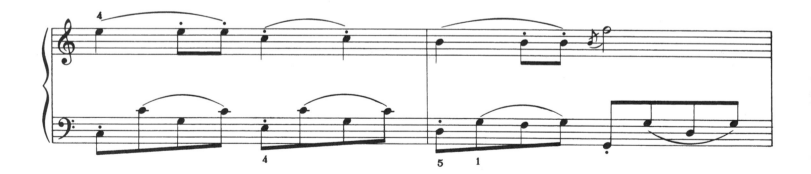

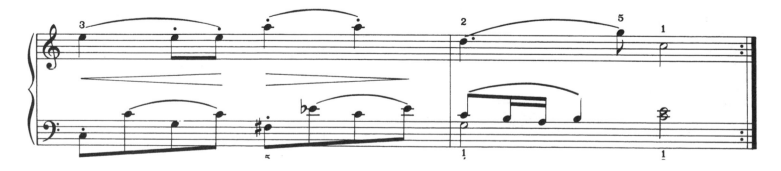

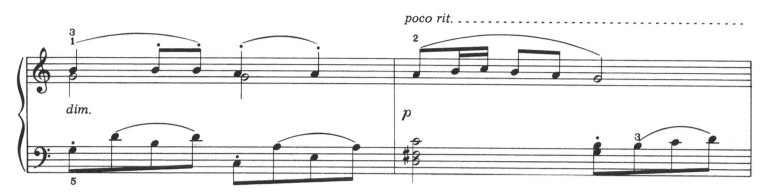

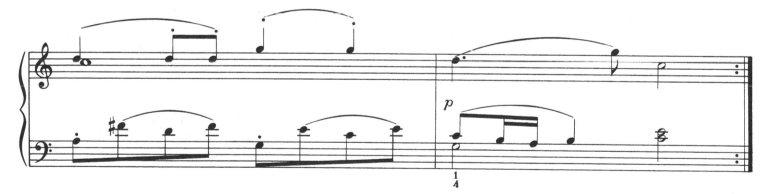

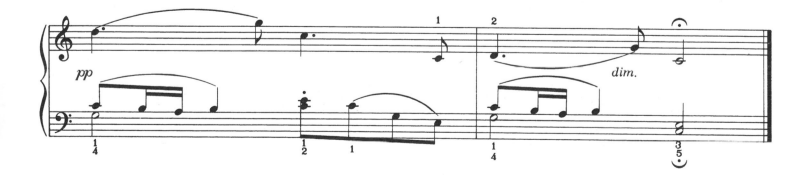

121

Theme
(from *The Unfinished Symphony*)

Music by Franz Schubert

Moderately

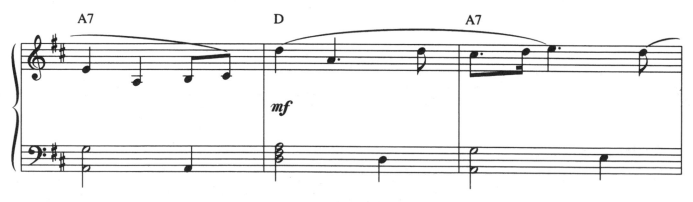

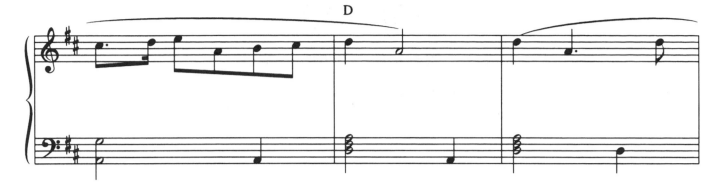

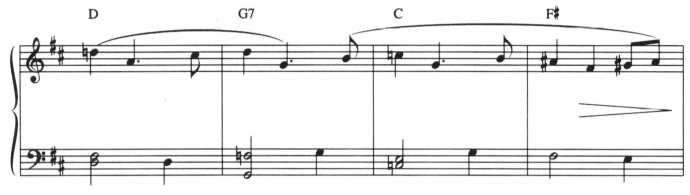

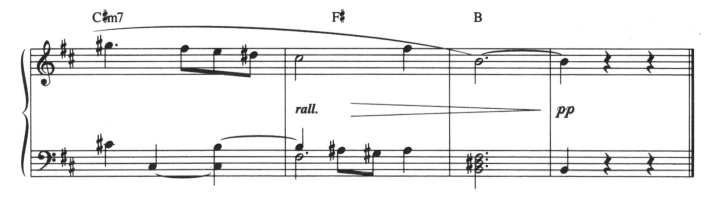

Waltz
(from *Die Fledermaus*)

Music by Johann Strauss II

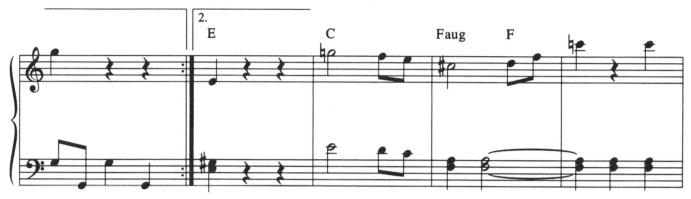

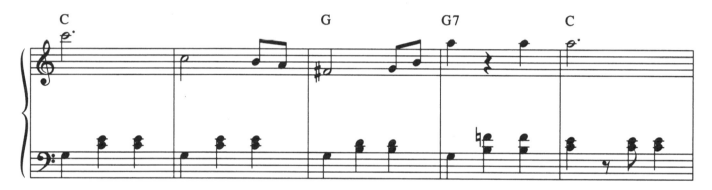

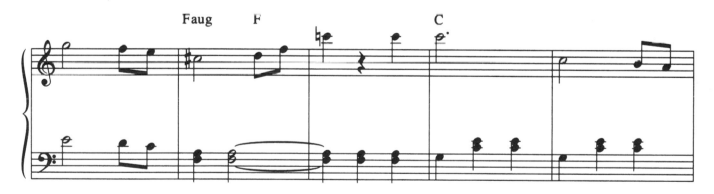

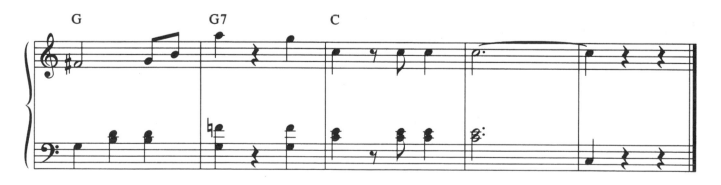

Morning Papers

Music by Johann Strauss II

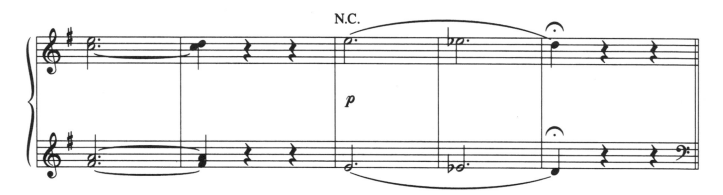

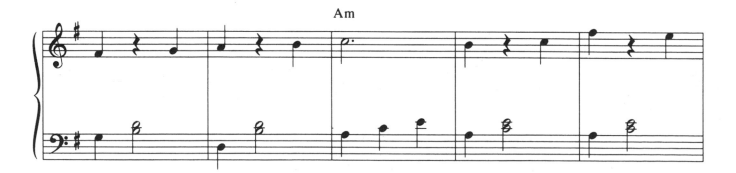

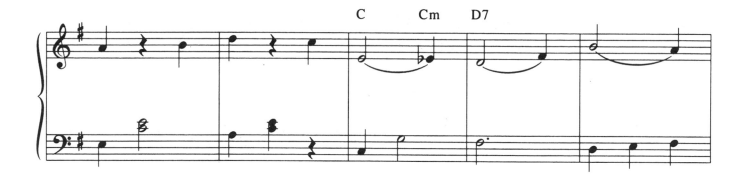

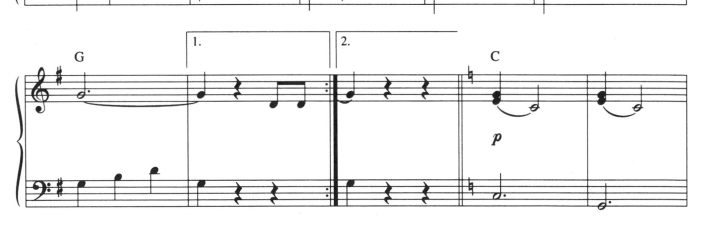

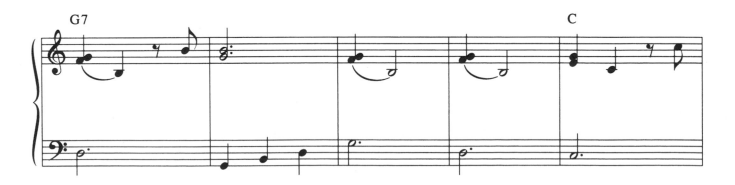

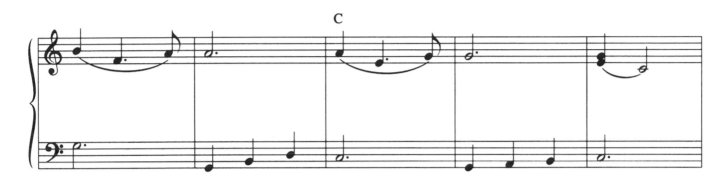

D.C. al Fine

Reve De Printemps

Music by Johann Strauss II

Bright waltz

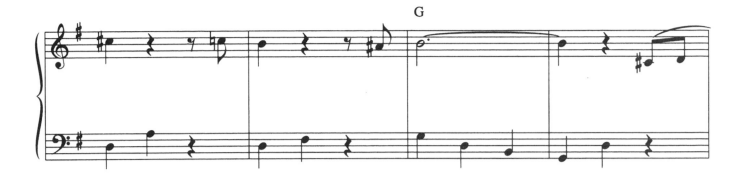

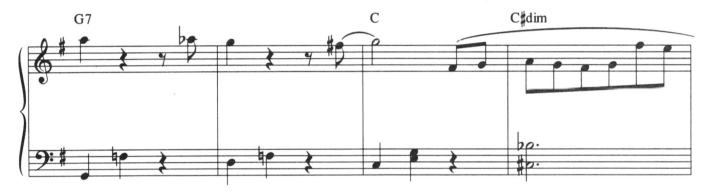

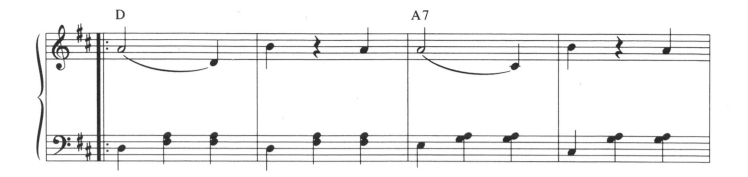

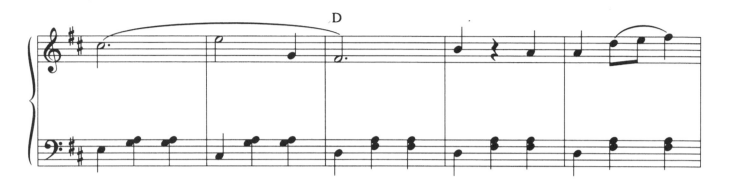

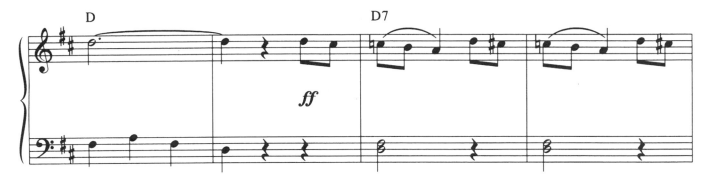

D.%. al Coda

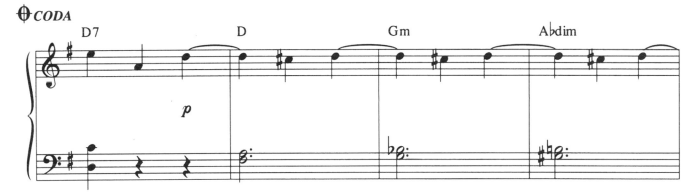

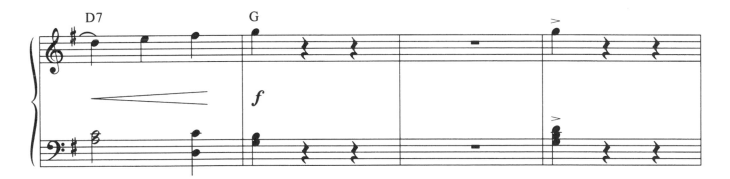

La Vie D'Artiste

Music by Johann Strauss II

Moderately

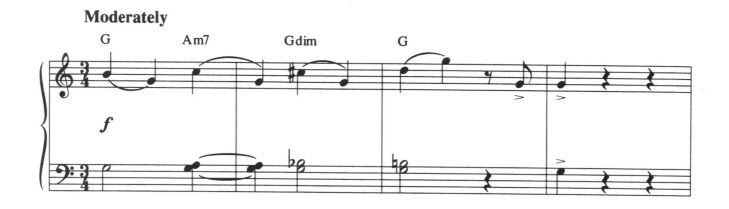

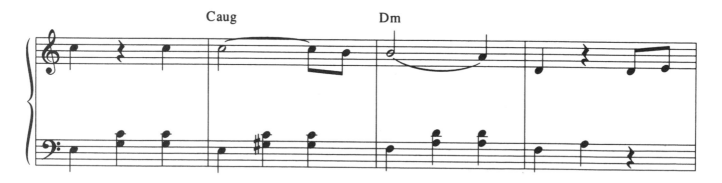

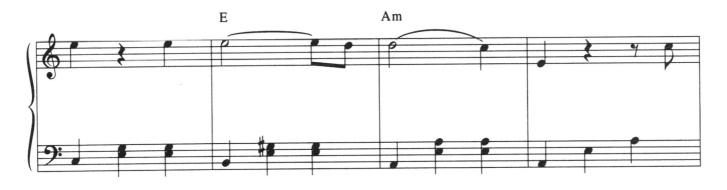

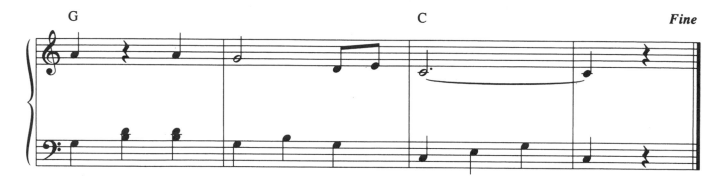

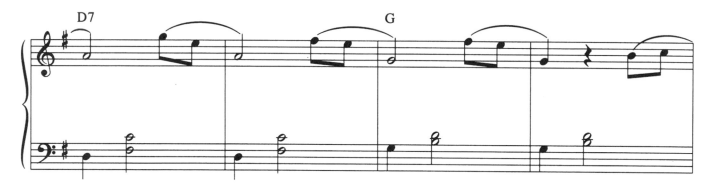

Tales From The Vienna Woods

Music by Johann Strauss II

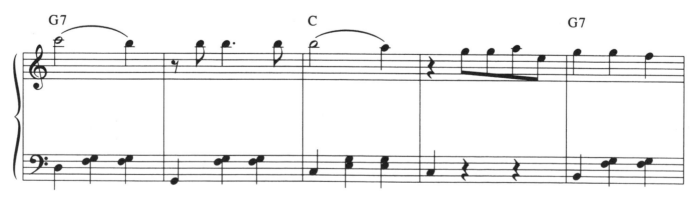

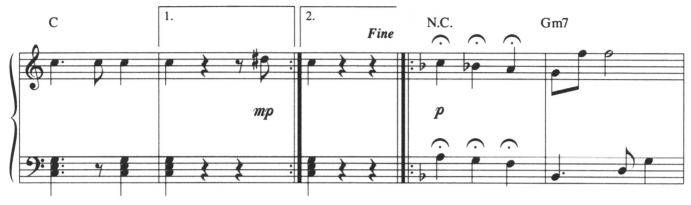

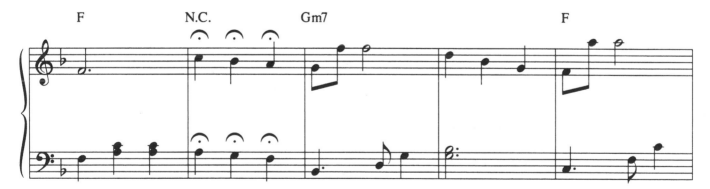

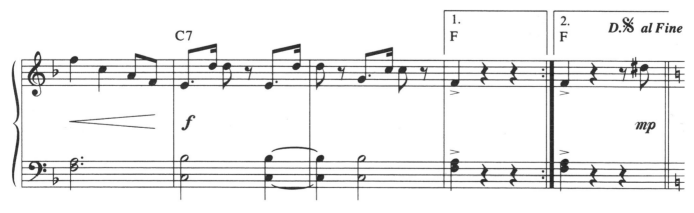

139

Vienna Blood

Music by Johann Strauss II

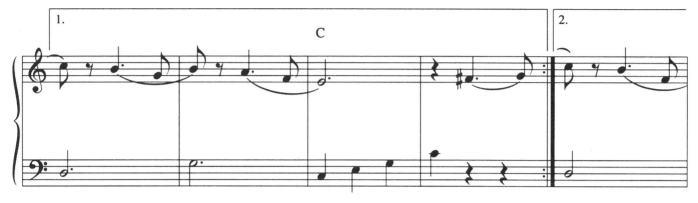

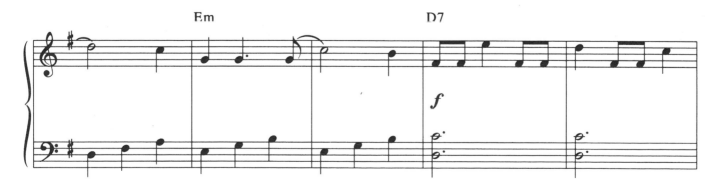

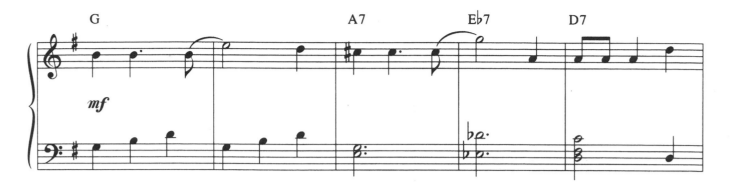

D.%. al Coda

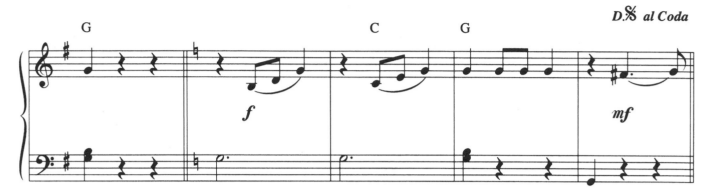

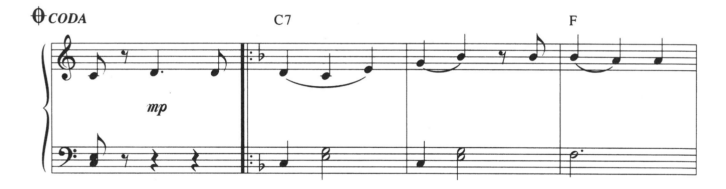

Village Swallows

Music by Josef Strauss

Moderately

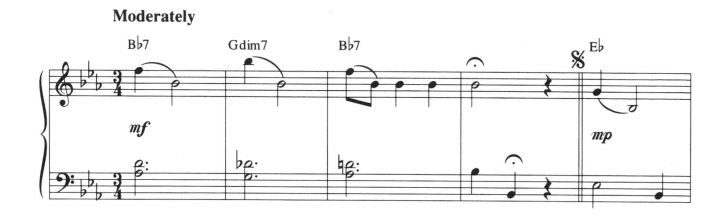

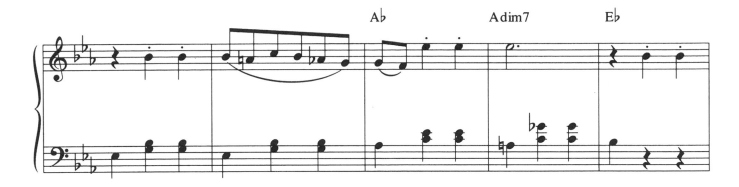

Ab   Adim7   Eb

Bb7   Eb

Bb7   Eb

Fm

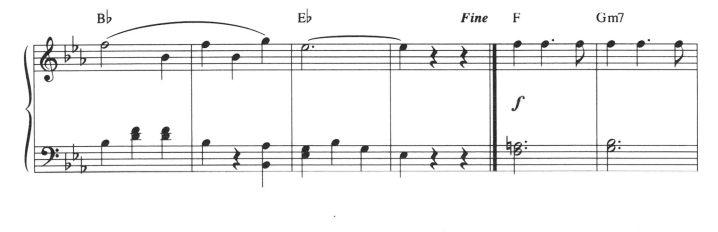

Bb   Eb   *Fine* F   Gm7

ƒ

145

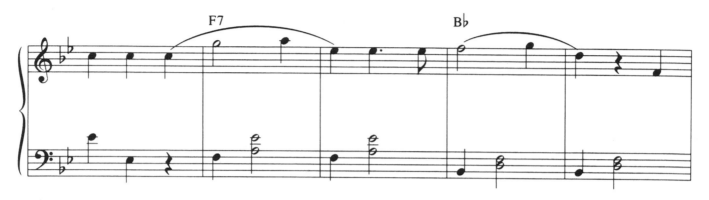

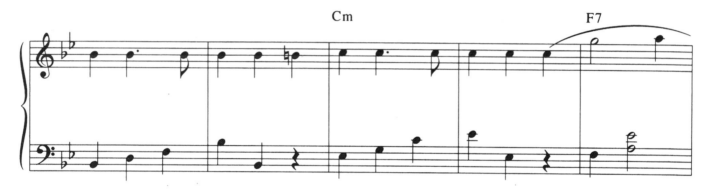

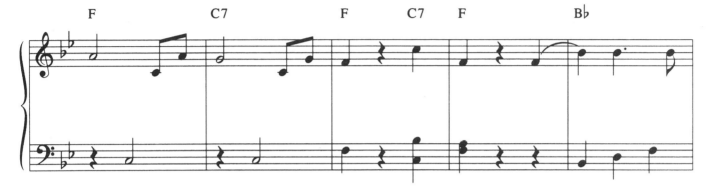

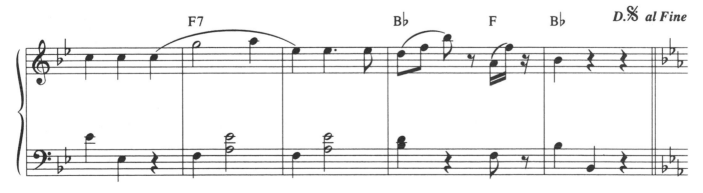

Theme
(from *Symphony No.5*)

Music by Pyotr Ilyich Tchaikovsky

Slowly and with feeling

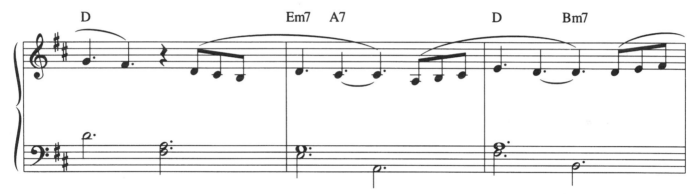

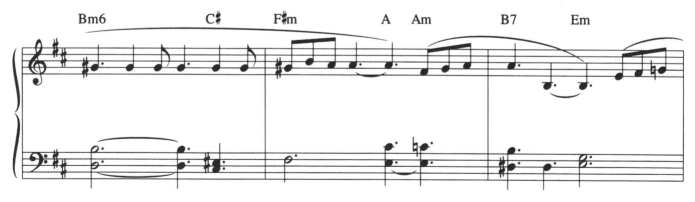

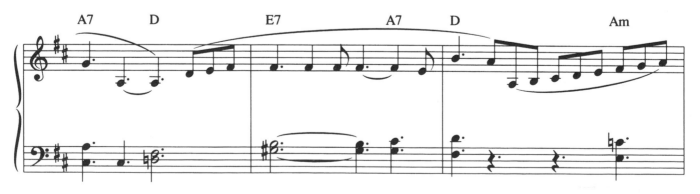

Force Of Destiny

Music by Giuseppe Verdi

Moderately slow

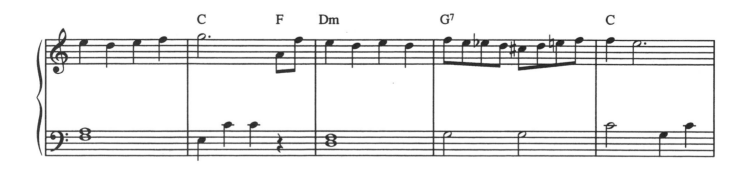

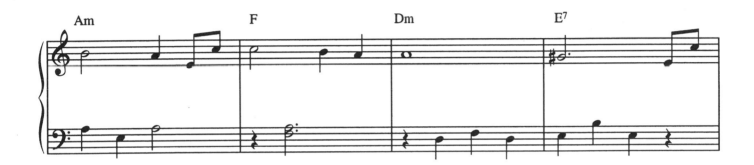

La Donna È Mobile
(from *Rigoletto*)

Music by Giuseppe Verdi

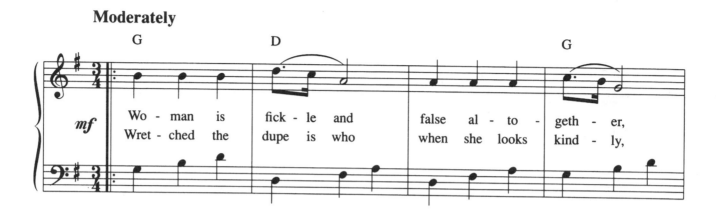

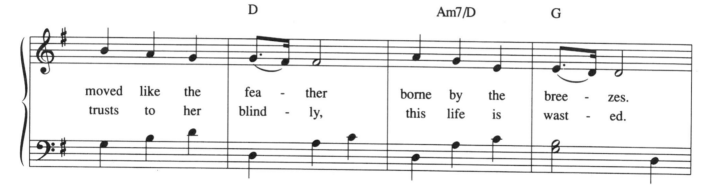

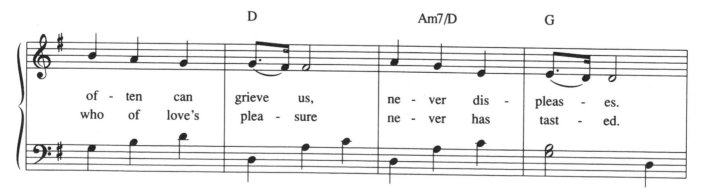

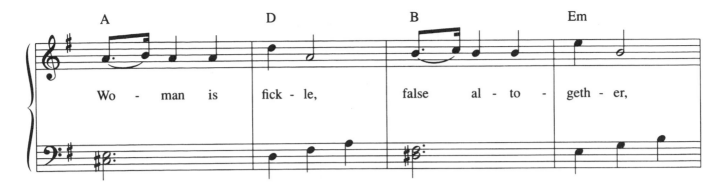

Wo - man is fick - le, false al - to - geth - er,

mov - ed like the fea - ther borne___ by the breezes,

borne___ by the breeze,

borne___ by___ the___ breeze. breeze.

Autumn
(from *The Four Seasons*)

Music by Antonio Vivaldi

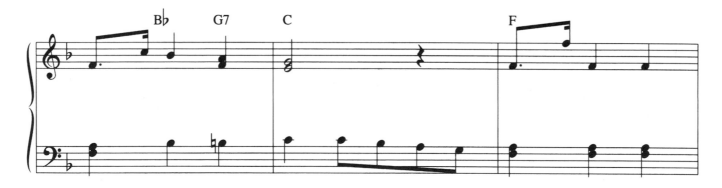

Bridal March
(from *Lohengrin*)

Music by Richard Wagner

Moderately

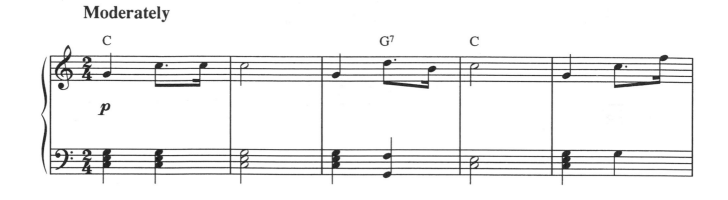

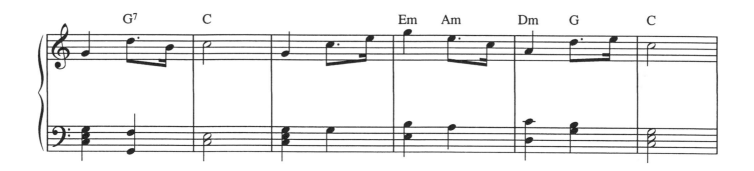

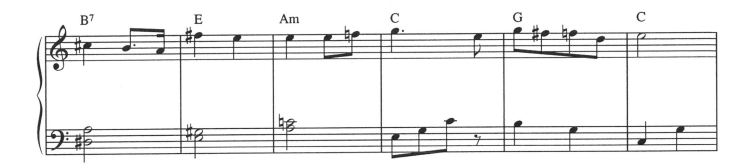

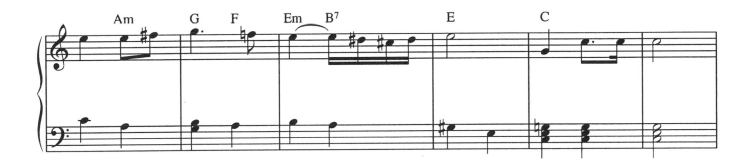

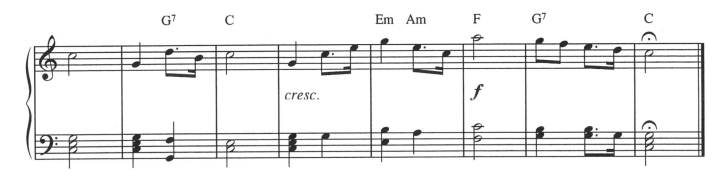

The Skater's Waltz

Music by Emile Waldteufel

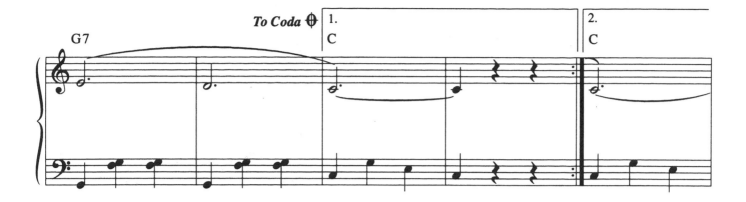

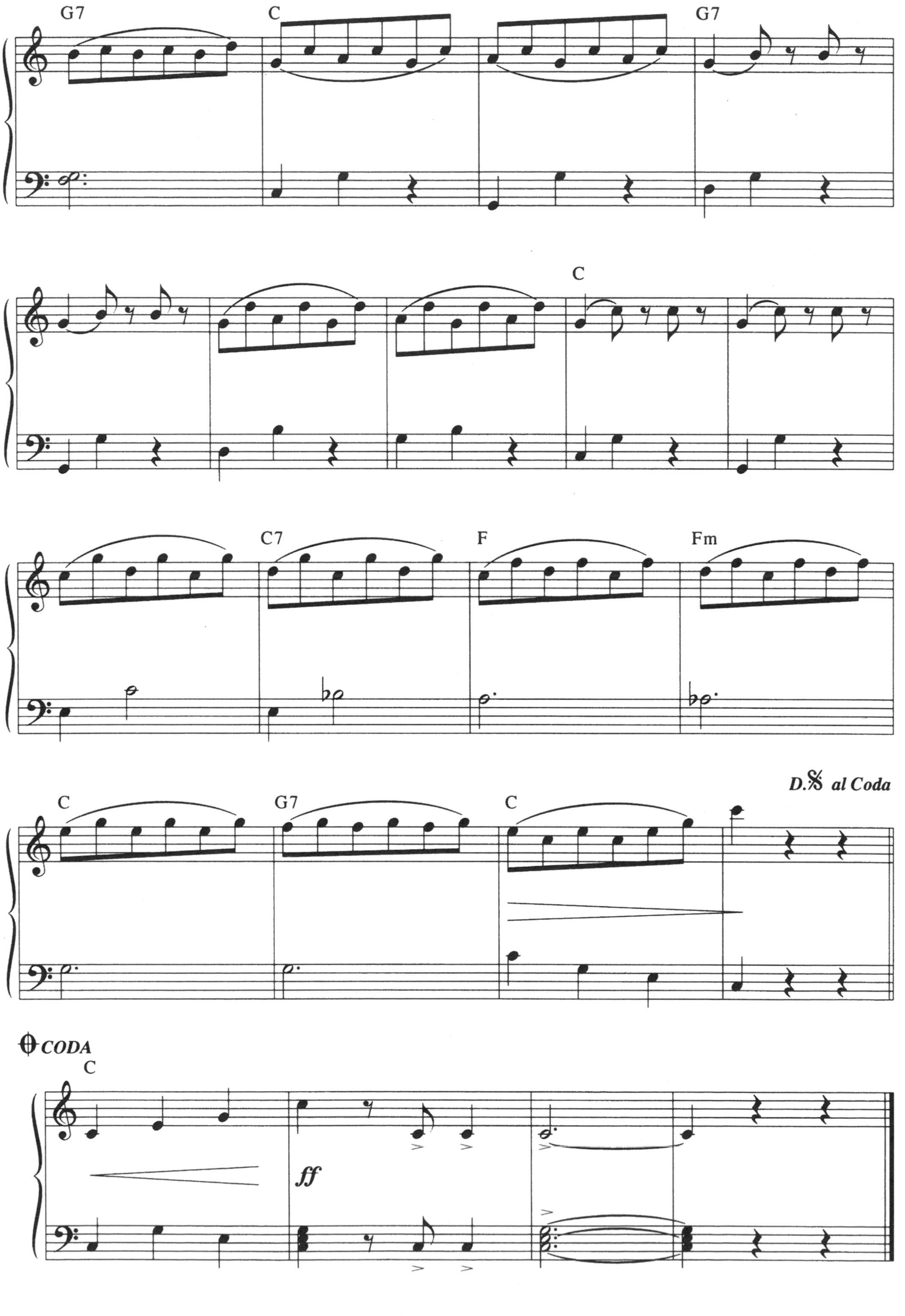

Printed in Malta by Progress Press Co. Ltd 11/09 (171838)